MW01714823

TRASH TO TREASURE CRAFTS

By
Jan Peak
and
Anna Hennig

STANDARD PUBLISHING

Library of Congress Cataloging-in-Publication Data

Peak, Jan, 1953-
Trash to treasure crafts / by Jan Peak and Anna Hennig.
p. cm.
Summary: Provides instructions for making a variety of crafts from empty milk containers, egg cartons, and other types of recycled waste.
ISBN 0-87403-890-1 : $8.99
1. Handicraft--Juvenile literature. 2. Waste products--Juvenile literature. [1. Handicraft. 2. Refuse and refuse disposal.]
I. Hennig, Anna Smith, 1960- . II. Title.
TT160.P38 1992
745.5--dc20 91-39789
CIP
AC

Published by The STANDARD PUBLISHING Company, Cincinnati, Ohio.
A Division of STANDEX INTERNATIONAL Corporation. Printed in U.S.A.

Printed on Recycled Paper

CONTENTS

TIPS FROM JANANNA

Hi! I'm glad to know that you are recycling materials too in order to help keep the earth God created beautiful! My book will help you create several neat projects from some of the recyclable materials.

Below is a list of all the recyclable materials you (or someone you know) will need to save to make my craft projects in this book. Remember, if you have any of the materials left over, either recycle them or save them for other kinds of craft projects.

My book will list and show you what you need for each project, step-by-step drawings to follow to make each project, and what the finished project should look like.

You will also find my "JANANNA TIPS" for almost every project in this book! My tips give suggestions of different ways you can make or use the craft.

There are also pattern pieces to help you make most of the projects in this book. All you have to do is to either trace or copy the patterns. But, remember, the pattern pieces are flat, so some pieces show where darts are needed to make the pattern fit on to objects. Ask an adult for help if needed.

Do not use scissors, X-Acto® Knife, or hot glue gun unless an adult helps you! If you do not want to use a hot glue gun, I recommend Instant Grrrip® from Bond® a super tacky glue. You can find it at your local craft store.

To remove stubborn labels and excess glue from plastic bottles, fill bottles with hot water and let set for five minutes. Then remove labels. If any of the labels or excess glue are left on the bottles (and there will be from my experience), use a cotton ball soaked with fingernail polish remover to remove remaining paper. My advice is to have an exhaust fan on when using the fingernail polish remover.

After painting plastic jugs, use a polyurethane spray to seal and protect your crafts.

God bless you and keep you safe!

RECYCLABLE MATERIALS NEEDED:

- aluminum foil
- butter or margarine lids: *large tub*
- cards: *greeting cards*
- catalogs: *department stores*
- coat hangers
- egg cartons: *cardboard*
- film canisters
- frozen juice containers: *lids*
- glass jars: *baby food*
- milk cartons: *plastic*
- paper scraps: *construction, tissue*
- paper tubes: *toilet paper*
- plastic bottles: *laundry detergent, liquid dish soap, 2-liter pop bottles, jug drinks*
- styrofoam meat trays
- tin cans
- yogurt cups

BIRD FEEDER

I need:

permanent marker

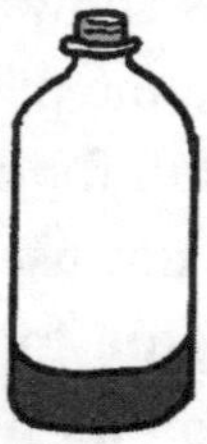

2-liter pop bottle

acrylic paint

paintbrush

coat hanger

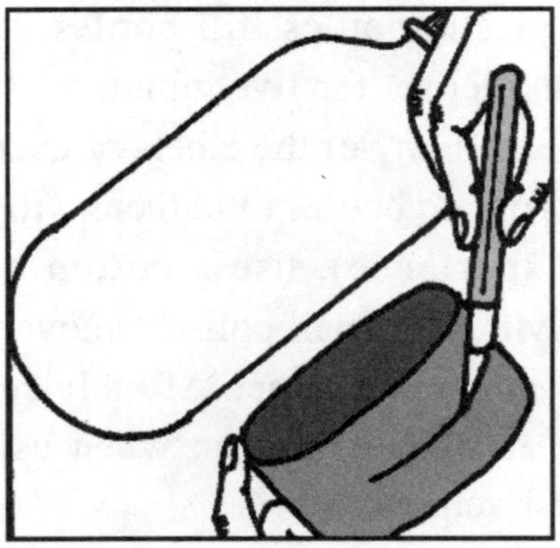

1 Steps one through four will need adult help. Soak bottle base in hot water for three to five minutes. Pull base off bottle carefully. Cut 1" from the top of the base.

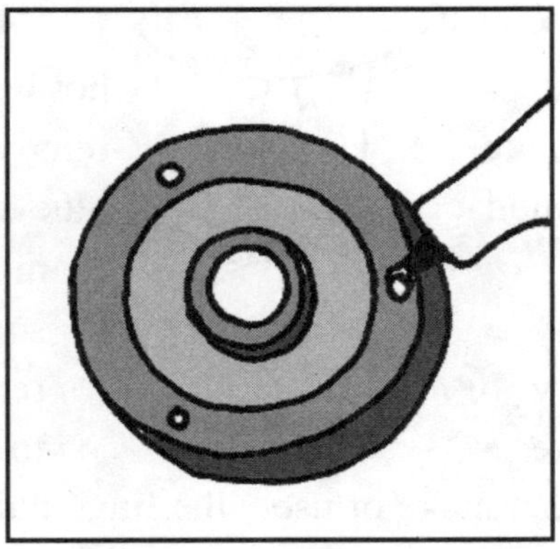

2 Cut a hole in the center of the base large enough for the mouth of the bottle to fit through it. Then plug any other holes in the base with hot glue.

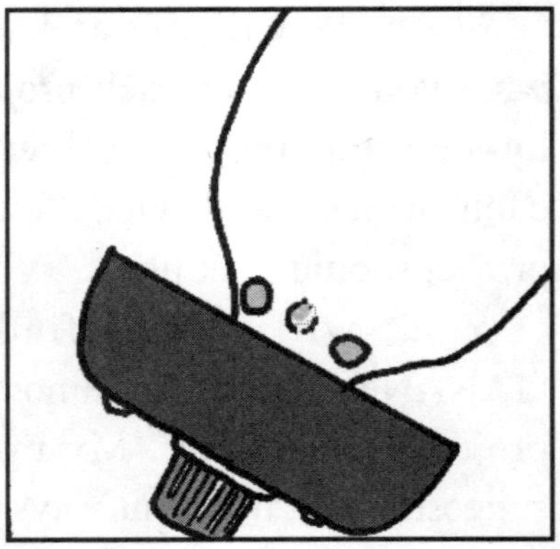

3 Cut three ½" holes with knife close to the mouth of the bottle to allow birdseed to fall into the base. Then put the mouth of the bottle through the hole of the base and glue together. Let dry.

JANANNA TIPS

Squirrels could possibly chew away the base of the feeder trying to get to the seed. If this happens, replace the chewed-up base with a new base following steps one through three.

wire cutters | scissors or X-Acto® knife | hot glue gun | birdseed

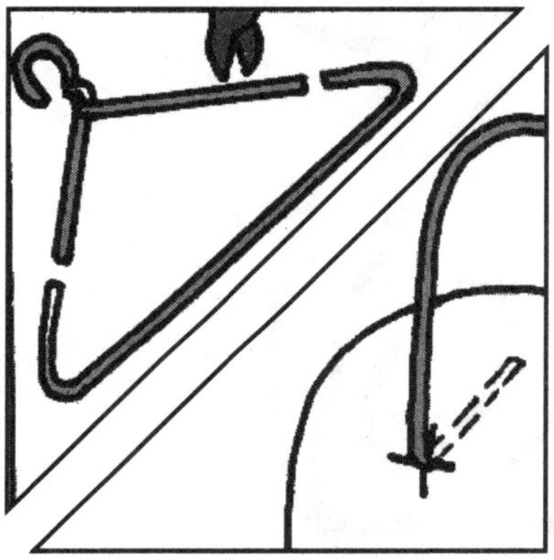

4 Cut the bottom of a hanger with wire cutters. Bend hanger into a **U** shape. Then cut two small **x**'s in the dome end of the bottle on opposite sides. Put ends of hanger into the **x**'s.

5 Cut out desired designs and trace designs onto bottle with a marker. Paint with desired colors. Let dry.

6 Fill bird feeder with birdseed and hang it out for the birds.

BIRD FEEDER DESIGNS

BIRD FEEDER DESIGNS

NOAH'S NAPKIN RINGS

I need:

toilet paper roll

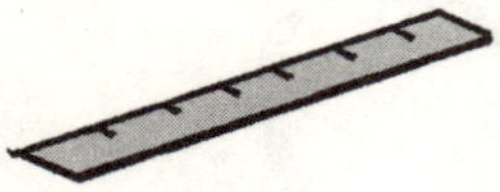

ruler

pencil

crayons or markers

scissors or X-Acto® knife

white glue

1 Measure, mark, and cut 2 ¼" sections of a toilet paper roll.

2 Color the desired patterns for your napkin rings. Then cut out the patterns.

3 Glue each head on one side of roll and tail on the other side of roll. Roll up a napkin and place inside of ring.

JANANNA TIPS

- These can make nice place setting name tags for parties.
- The toilet paper rolls may be painted to add color to the napkin rings.

NOAH'S NAPKIN RINGS PATTERNS

BEAR HEADS
AND
TAILS

MONKEY HEADS
AND
TAILS

RABBIT HEADS
AND
TAILS

NOAH'S NAPKIN RINGS PATTERNS

LION HEADS
AND
TAILS

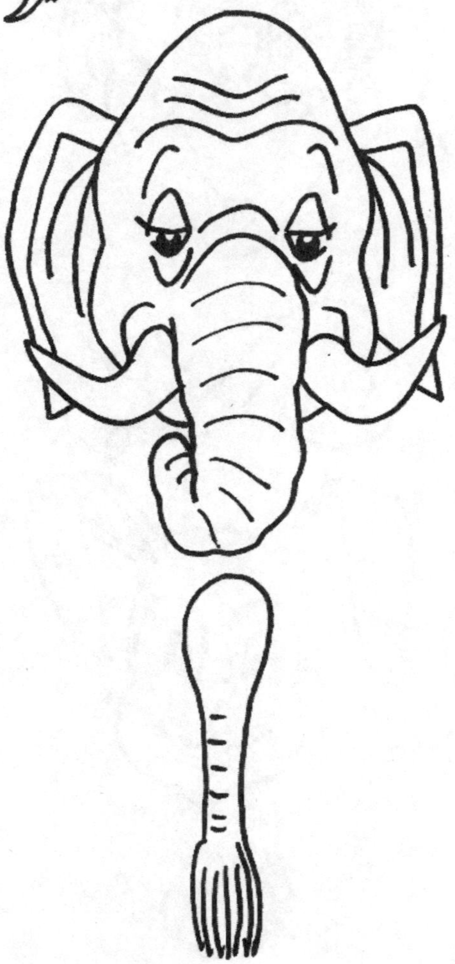

ELEPHANT
HEADS
AND
TAILS

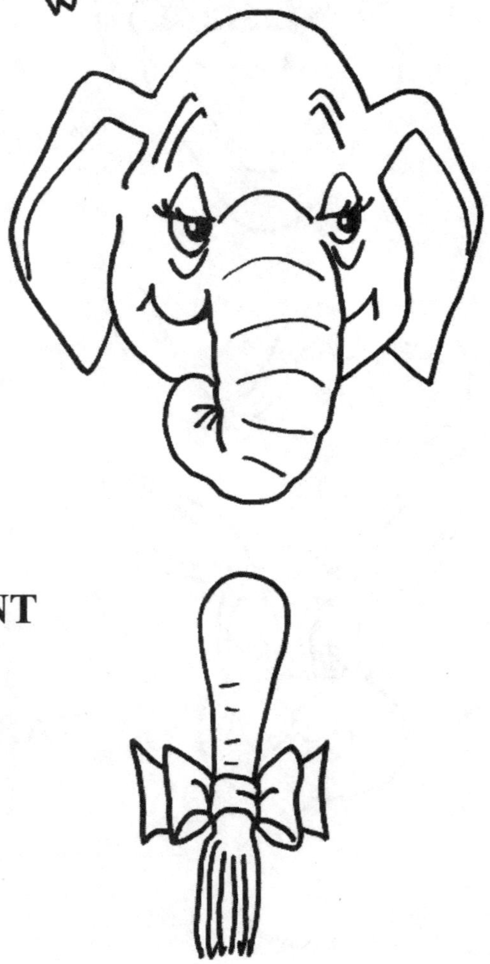

"JESUS LOVES ME" HEART

I need:

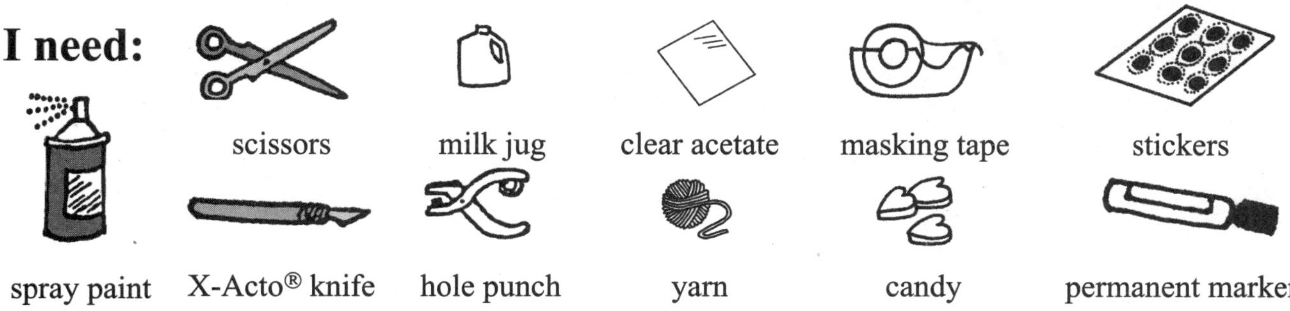

1 Trace pattern with marker on jug and acetate and cut out. Paint jug heart desired color and let dry. Place a sticker onto the center of acetate heart.

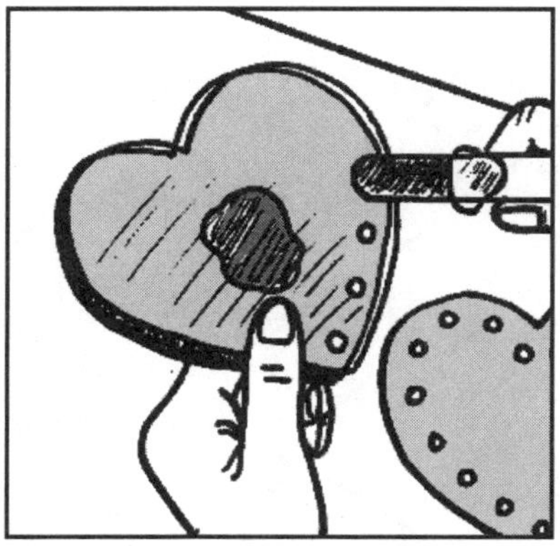

2 Put together jug heart and acetate heart. Punch holes ½" apart around entire heart.

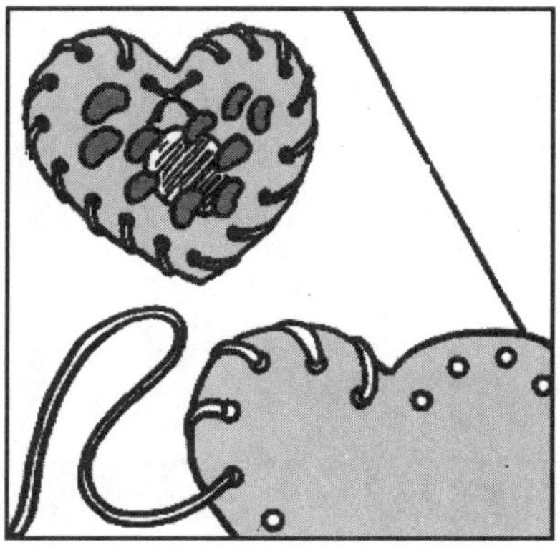

3 Cut 36" of yarn and wrap one end with tape tightly. Tie other end through one of the holes at the top of the heart and tie in a knot. Lace yarn around heart shape, but leave a 2" opening. Fill heart with desired amount of candy. Finish lacing heart and tie yarn in a knot.

JANANNA TIPS

Be creative with your shapes! I have also given you a bell pattern to make.

HEART PATTERN

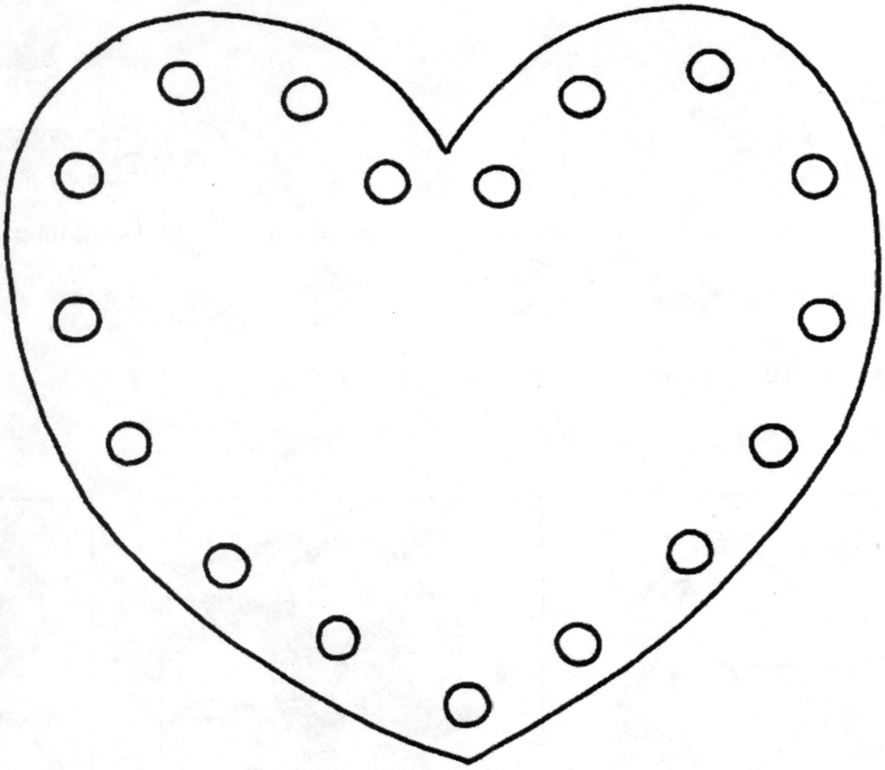

BELL PATTERN

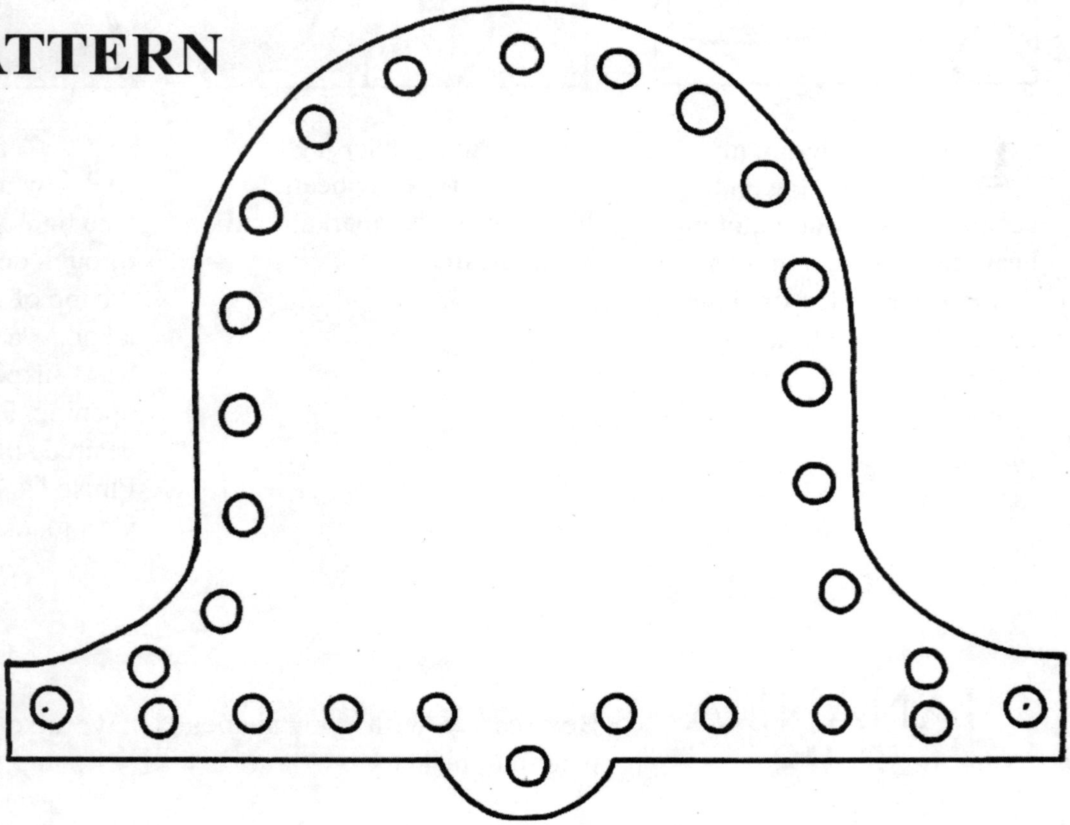

LOVE BUG CANISTER

I need:

film canister | one 1" pom-pom | two 5mm eyes | one pearl tip stamen | hot glue gun or white glue

1 Glue pom-pom onto film canister lid and let dry.

2 Glue eyes onto pom-poms and let dry.

3 Fold flower stamen in half. Then glue stamen down into pom-pom to look like antennas and let dry. Fill with candy or small nick-nacks.

JANANNA TIPS

These are great to use in piñatas so each child gets the same amount of candy.

BUMBLEBEE

I need:

cardboard egg carton

black and yellow acrylic paint

hot glue gun

pearl tip stamen

scissors

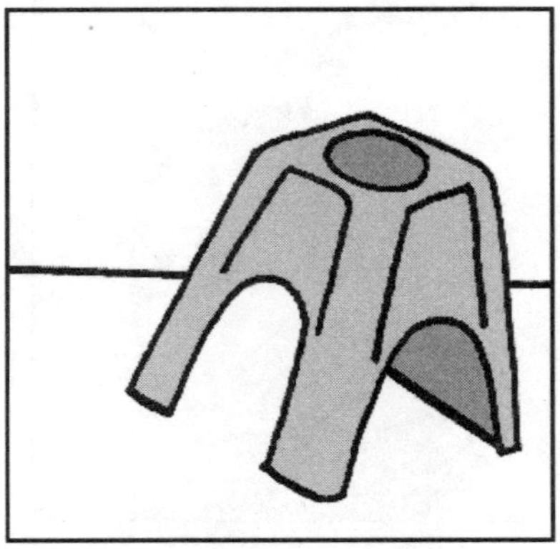

1 Cut out a one-cup section from the egg carton.

2 Paint black and yellow stripes on egg carton cup. Let dry.

3 Trace and cut out wings from pattern onto light blue construction paper.

JANANNA TIPS

The bee can be changed to a butterfly by painting the egg carton cup brown and using a brown pom-pom and the butterfly wings on page 20.

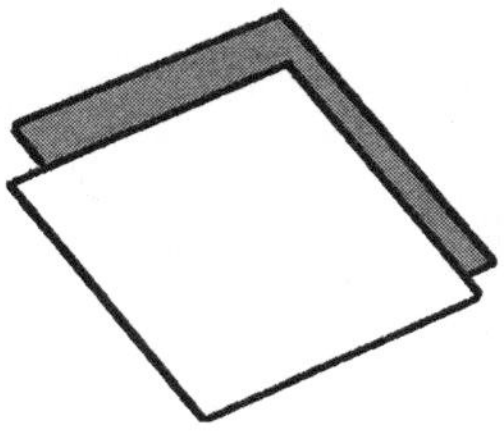

light blue
construction paper

paint brush

one black
1" pom-pom

two 5mm eyes

4 Glue wings and pom-pom for head onto egg carton. Let dry.

5 Glue eyes onto pom-pom. Let dry.

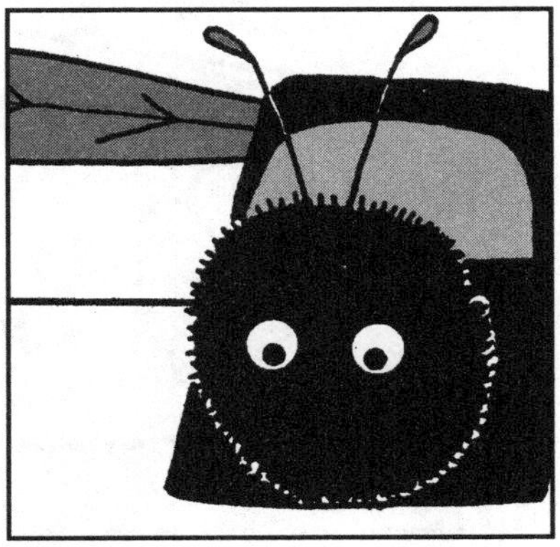

6 Fold stamen in half. Then glue into pom-pom and let dry.

DAISY

I need:

milk jug

one ½" yellow pom-pom

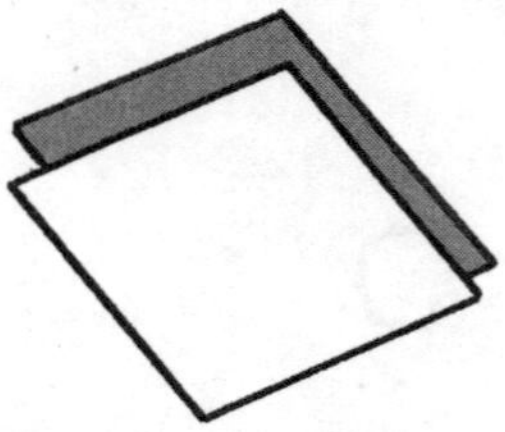

green construction paper

paint brush

green acrylic paint

$\frac{7}{16}$" dowel rod (18" long)

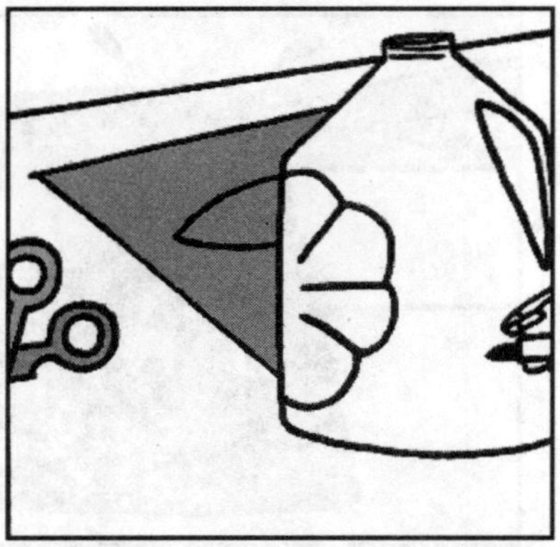

1 Trace and cut out daisy pattern from milk jug. Then trace and cut out leaves pattern from green construction paper.

2 Glue yellow pom-pom on center of daisy. Let dry.

3 Paint the dowel rod green and let dry.

JANANNA TIPS

For a unique table decoration, another daisy can be made and glued on the back side of the dowel rod. Also, add the butterfly to this daisy.

12" pipe cleaner

masking tape

scissors

clay flower pot filled with moss grass

hot glue gun

4 Glue one end of pipe cleaner to center of the bumblebee. Then tape other end of wire to the top of dowel rod.

5 Glue daisy to dowel rod and let dry.

6 Glue leaves to base of dowel rod and let dry. Then place dowel rod in hole of flower pot and glue in place. Fill flower pot with moss grass or artificial grass.

BUMBLEBEE WINGS PATTERNS

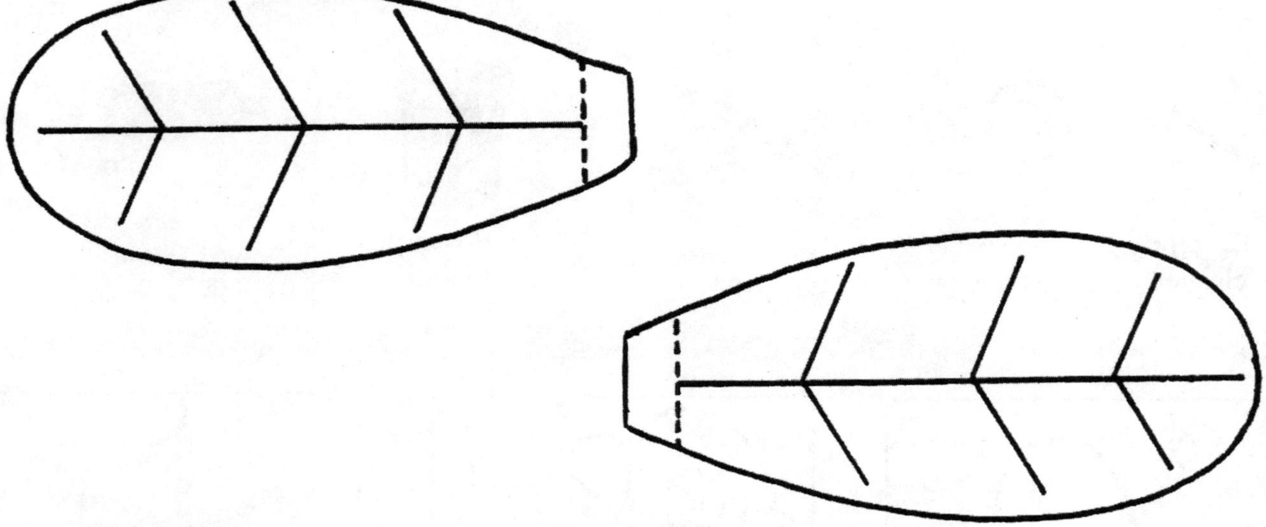

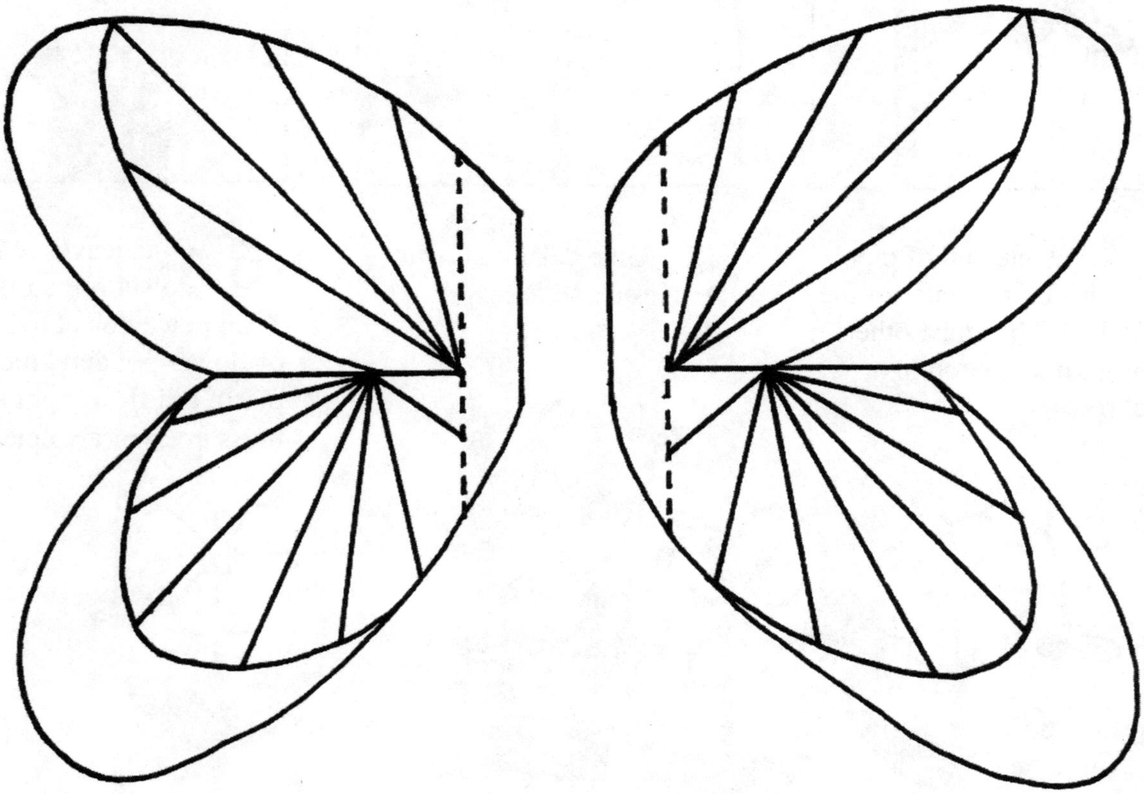

BUTTERFLY WINGS PATTERNS

LEAVES PATTERN

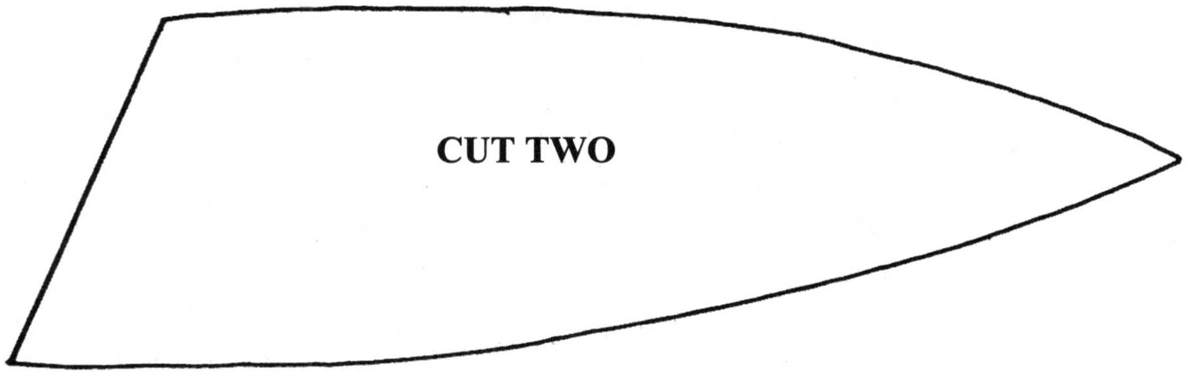

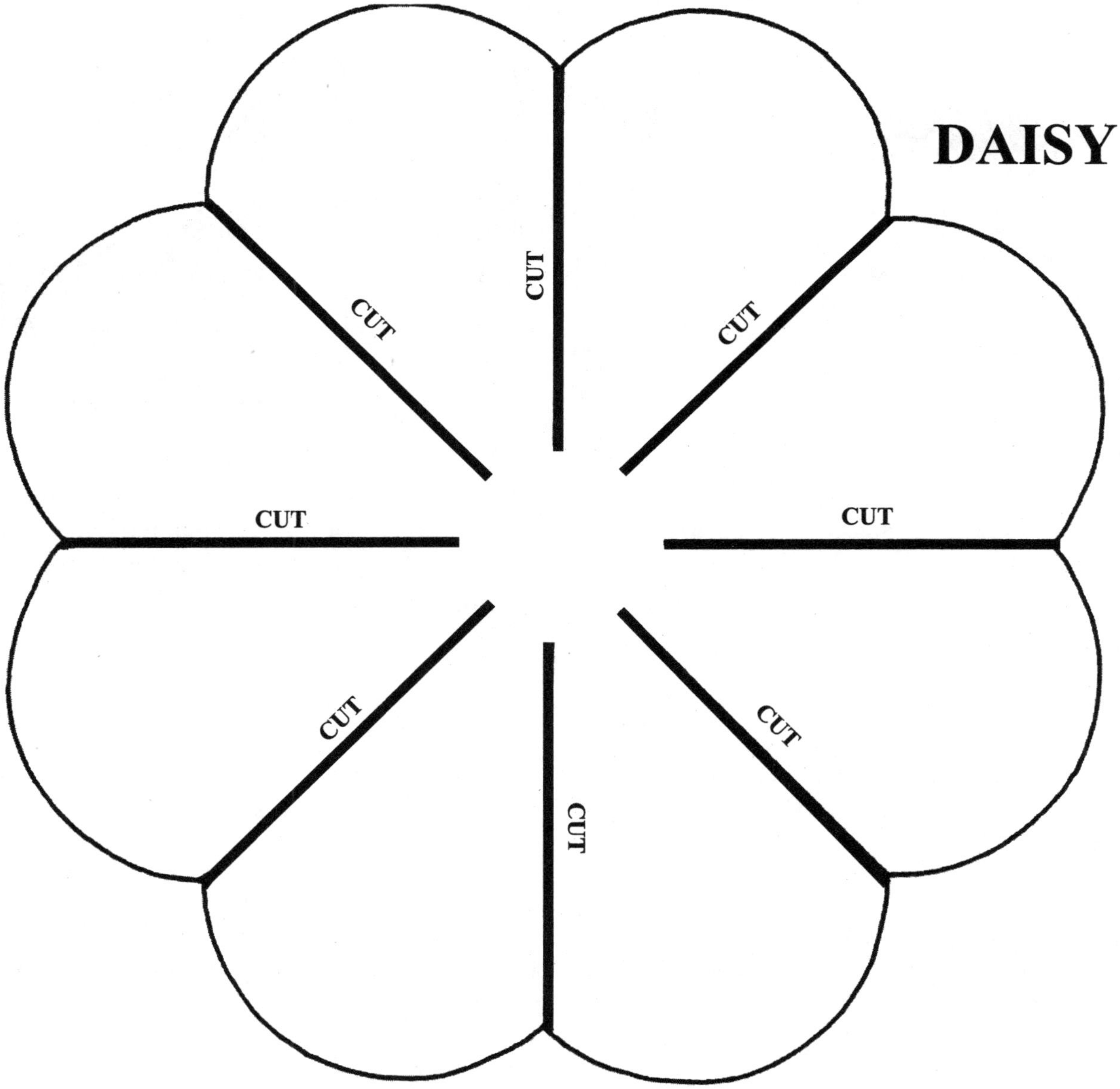

DAISY

GOLIATH STOMPERS

I need:

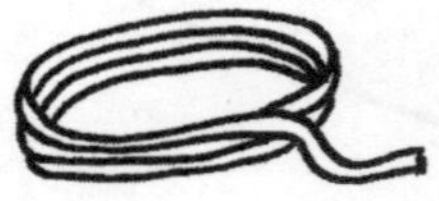

rope

two tin cans

scissors

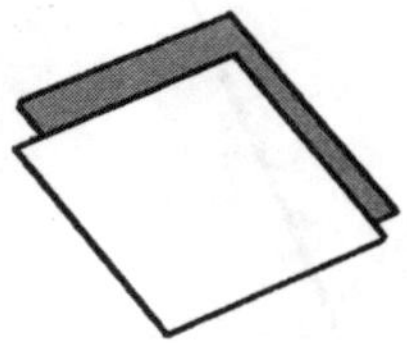

construction paper

1 Punch a hole in each top side of cans with a can opener.

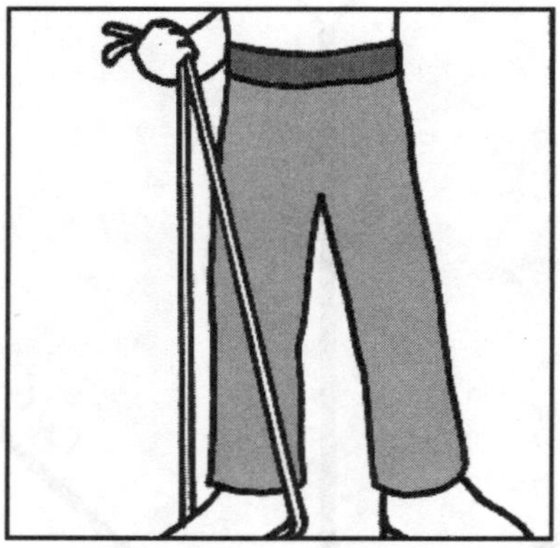

2 Hold rope at waist and extend it down under your foot and back up to your waist again. Cut rope. Then cut a second rope the same length as the first rope.

3 From the outside of the can, put both ends of rope through the holes and tie in a knot, making sure the knot is inside the can.

JANANNA TIPS	You will need to practice in the grass first until you get your balance.

spray paint

stencil designs

can opener

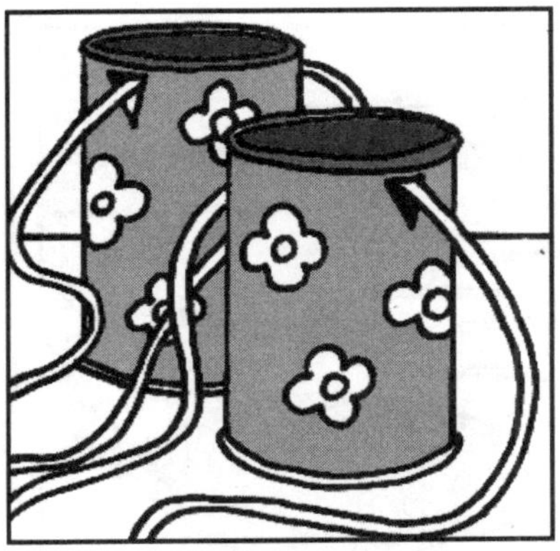

4 Decorate the cans with shapes of construction paper or spray paint stencil designs on the cans.

5 Step up carefully onto cans as you hold tightly to both ropes and begin walking.

CREATION CHIMES

I need:

metal juice lids

large 1 lb. butter lid

hammer

one small nail

one large nail

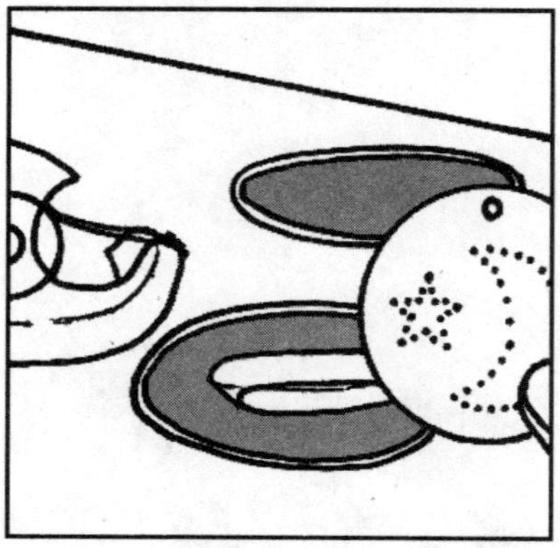

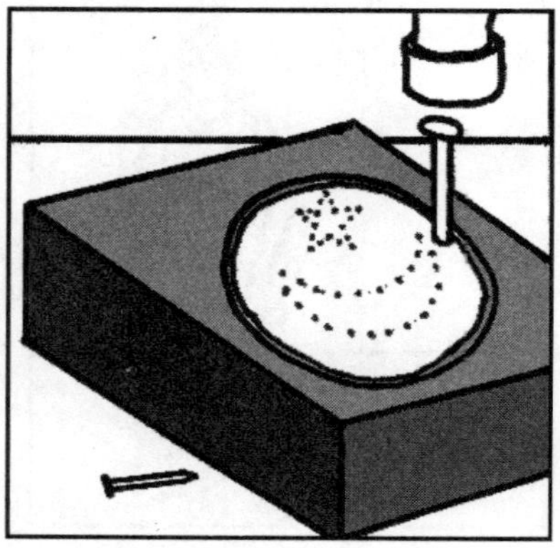

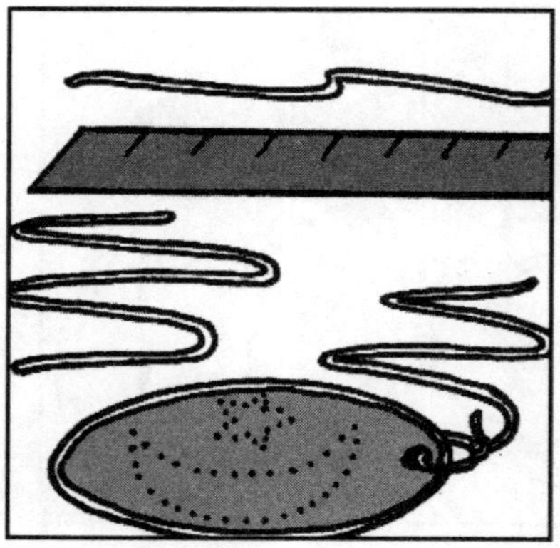

1 Cut out designs and tape each one to a metal juice lid.

2 Place one juice lid on a block of wood. By following the outline, make holes in the lid by lightly hammering the small nail. Then use a larger nail to make a hole in the top of the lid for the string. Repeat this step for the rest of the designs.

3 Cut eight 12" pieces of string. Then put one end of string through the top hole of each lid and tie in a knot.

JANANNA TIPS

- Hang the string from a doorknob to keep the string from becoming tangled.
- If chimes are hung outdoors, spray chimes with a clear finish to prevent metal from rusting.

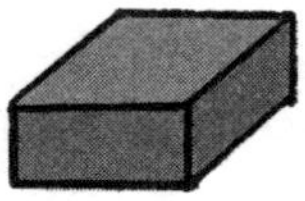

block of wood

string

hole punch

pipe cleaner

cellophane tape

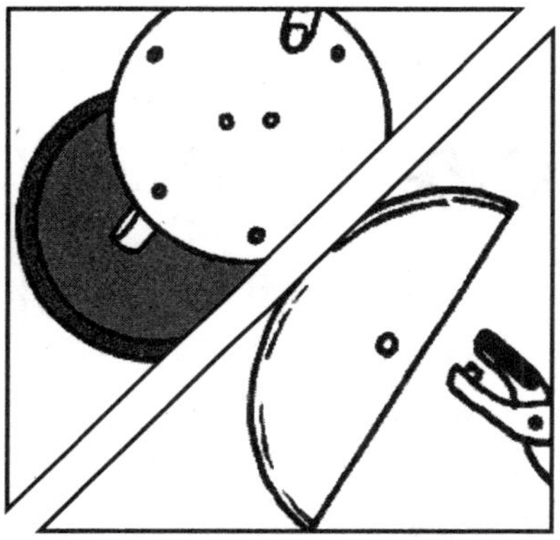

4 Cut and tape pattern on butter lid and punch holes where marked. For center holes, fold butter lid in half and punch holes.

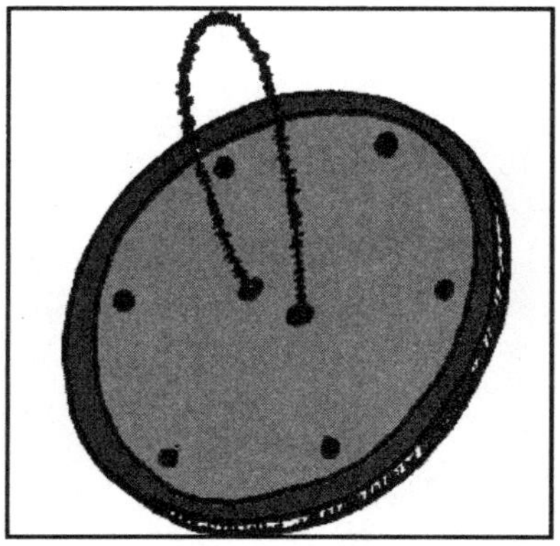

5 Bend a pipe cleaner in a **U** shape and place ends through the center holes of butter lid. Then twist ends together.

6 Tie the "sun" design to the bottom hole of "God." Then tie "God" to the center holes of the butter lid. Take the last six designs and tie to outside holes of butter lid.

CREATION CHIMES PATTERNS

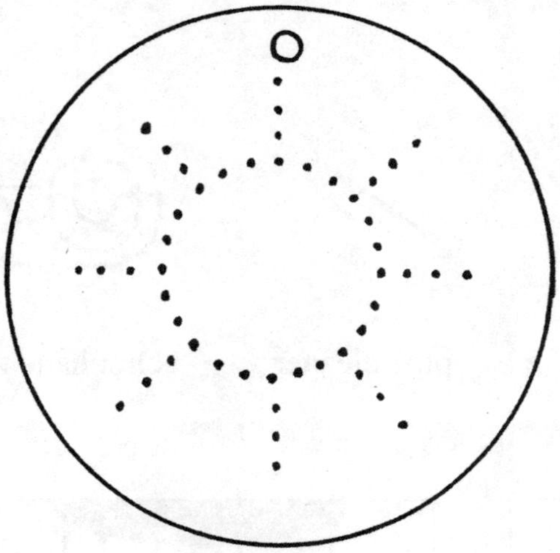

SUN

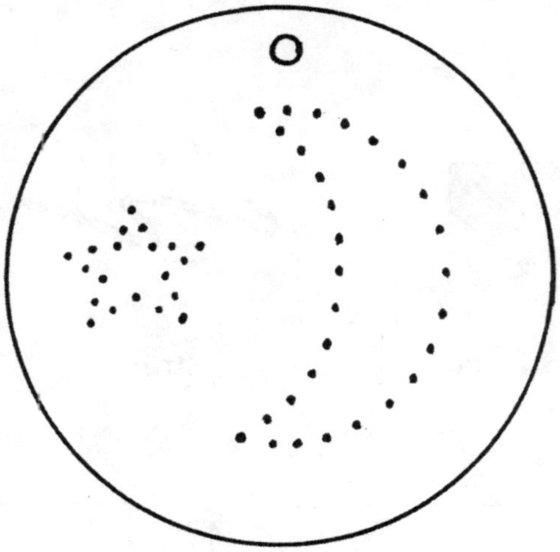

STAR AND MOON

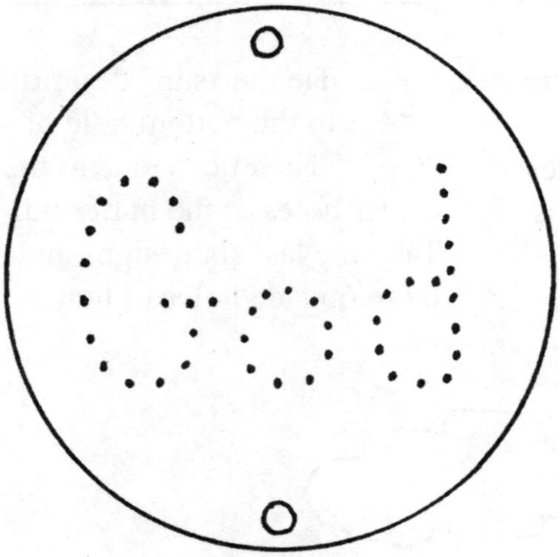

GOD

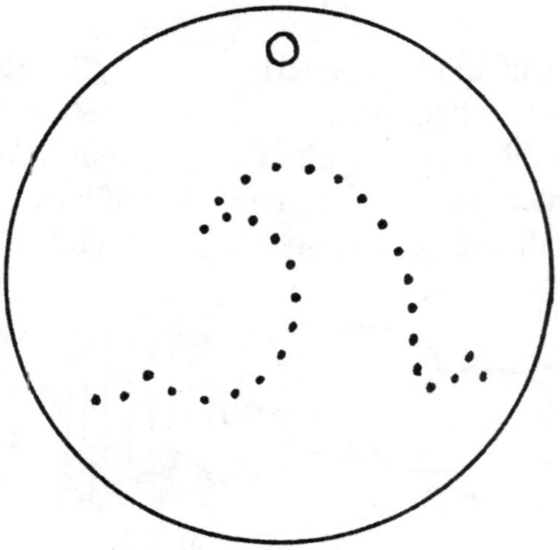

WATER

CREATION CHIMES PATTERNS

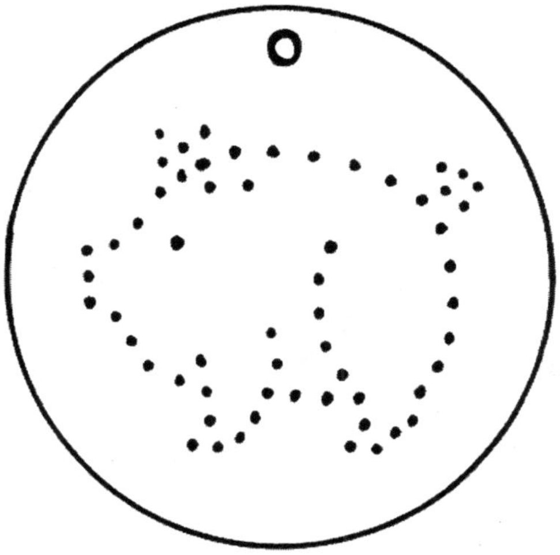

ANIMAL

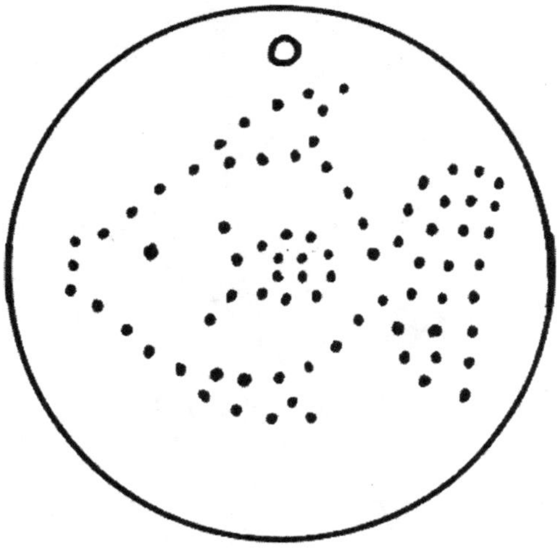

FISH

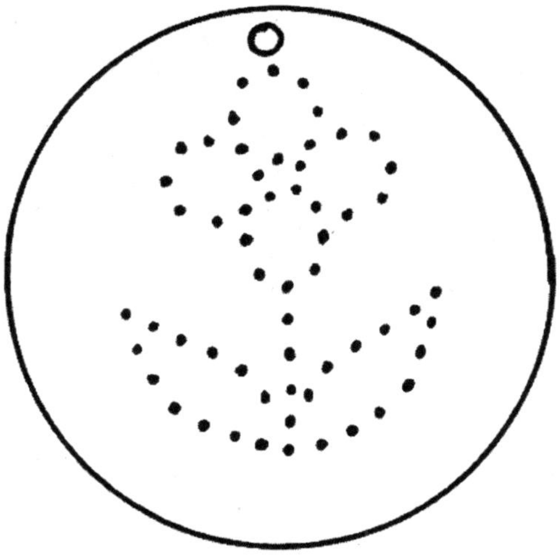

PLANTS

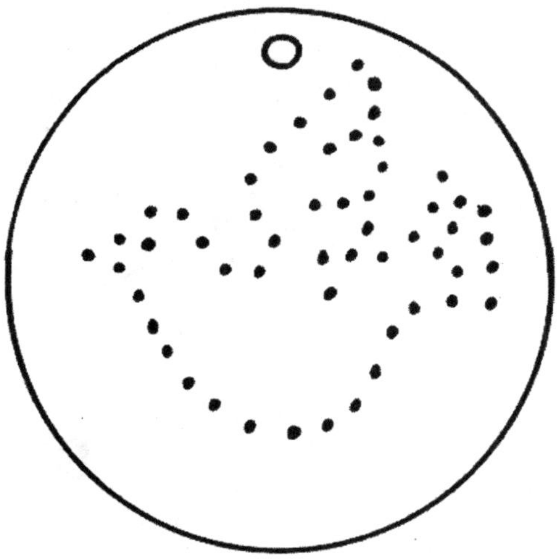

WATER

CREATION CHIMES PATTERNS

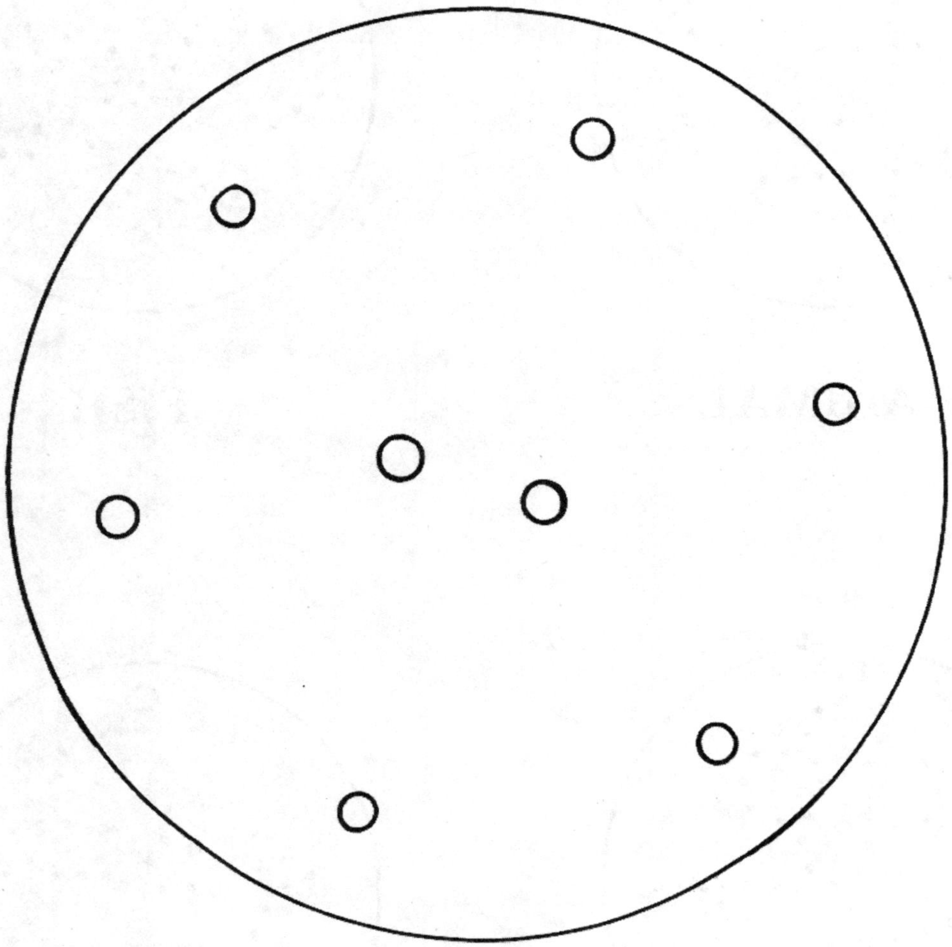

BUTTER LID

RABBIT

I need:

scissors

permanent marker

two ½" white pom-poms

two 5mm craft eyes

X-Acto® knife

one 5mm pink pom-pom

jug

one ¾" white pom-pom

1 Trace pattern with marker onto jug.

2 Cut out form from jug with scissors or knife. (Ask for adult help.)

3 Glue eyes, 5mm pom-pom for nose, and two 1/2 " white pom-poms for cheeks to face, and let dry. Then glue 3/4" pom-pom onto back for tail and let dry.

JANANNA TIPS

I like to use the top rim of the jug as a pedestal for Easter eggs. Simply cut off the top rim of the jugs. Decorate the rim with ribbon, lace, and sequins.

RABBIT PATTERN

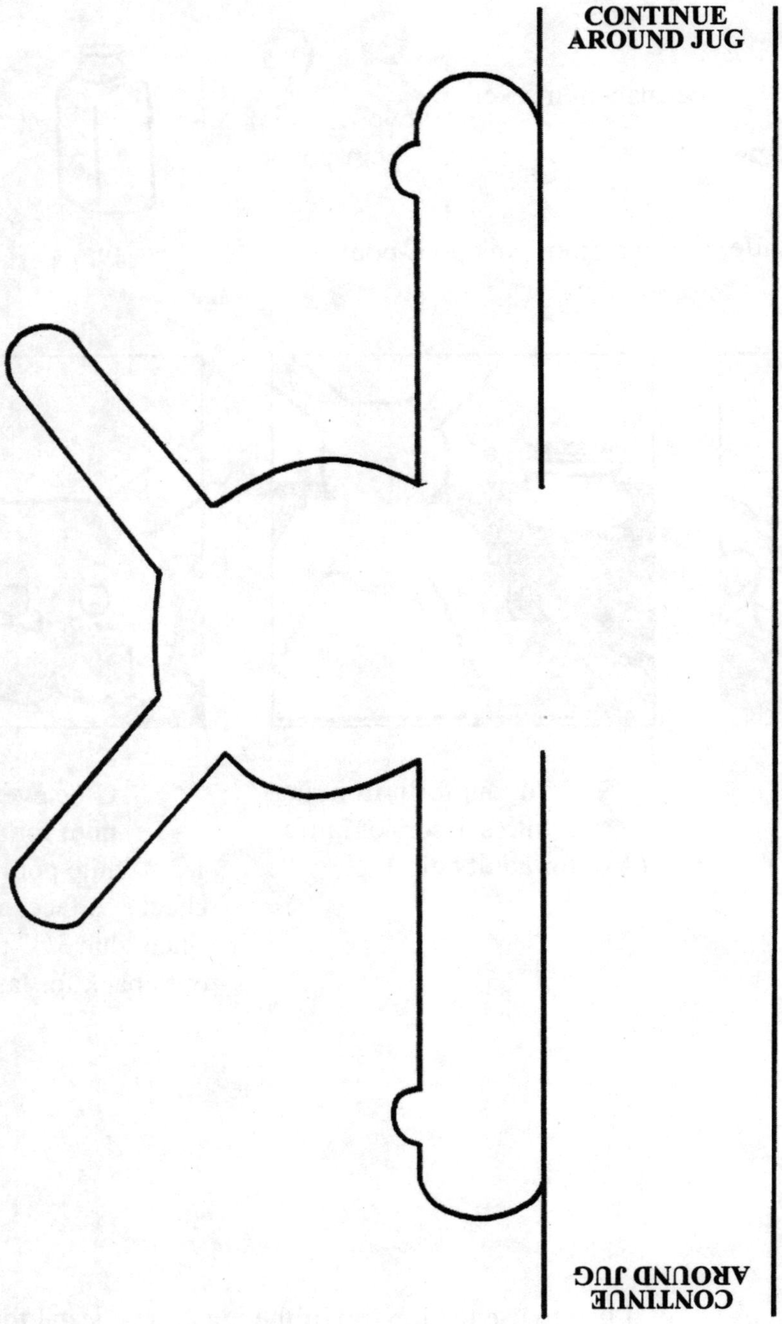

RAINBOW

I need:

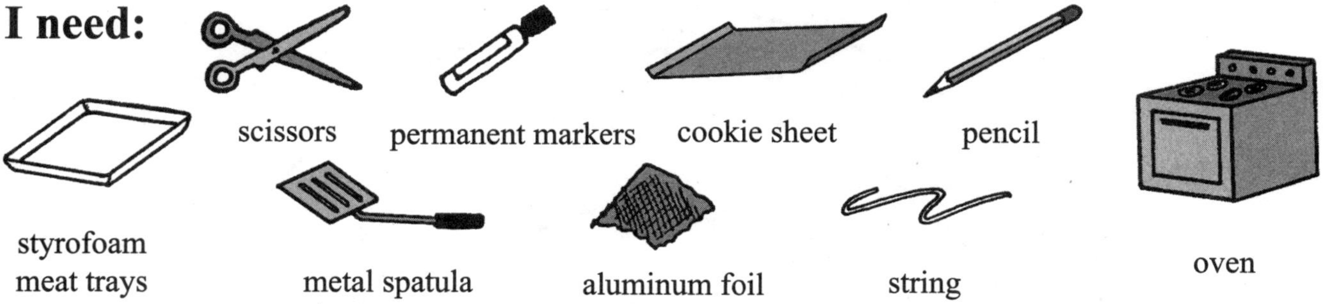

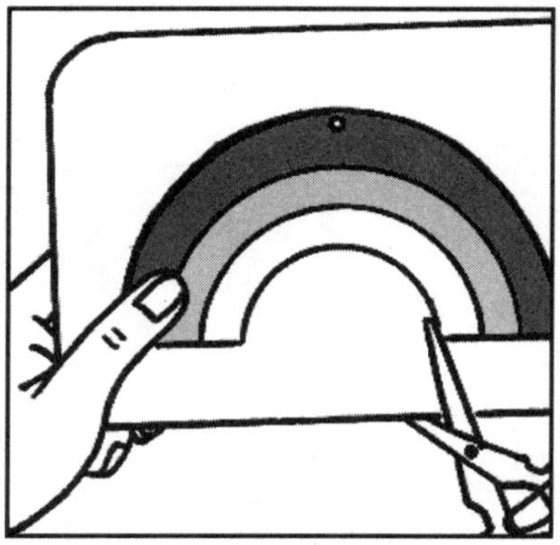

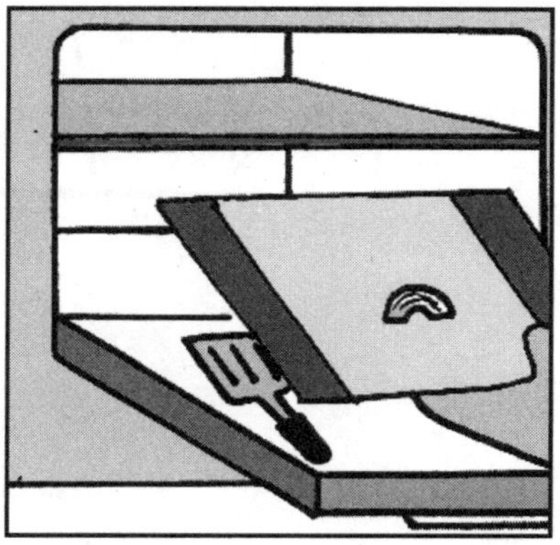

1 Trace rainbow pattern onto meat tray. Color in with permanent markers.

2 Cut out rainbow carefully with scissors. Poke a hole in rainbow, using the pencil tip, to make a necklace.

3 Place rainbow on a foil-covered cookie sheet. Put cookie sheet in oven at 300° for three minutes. (If piece has curled, have adult flatten with a metal spatula.) Remove cookie sheet from oven and let cool. The rainbow will be smaller and harder. Add a string to make a necklace.

JANANNA TIPS

- Have ventilation fan going to keep odor down.
- Shapes can be made into magnets or pins. Pinbacks may be found at your local craft store.
- For true colors, make sure to use white meat trays.

RAINBOW PATTERN

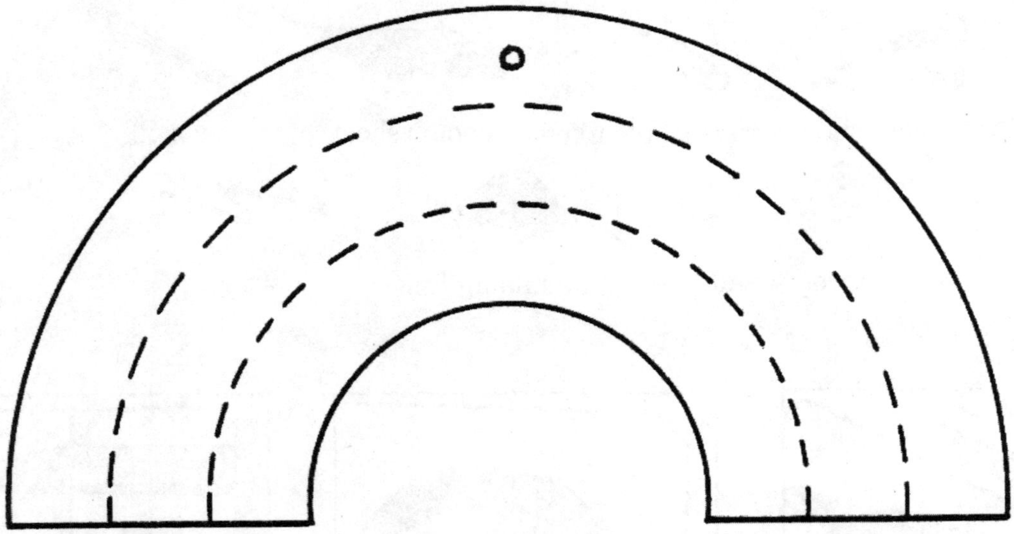

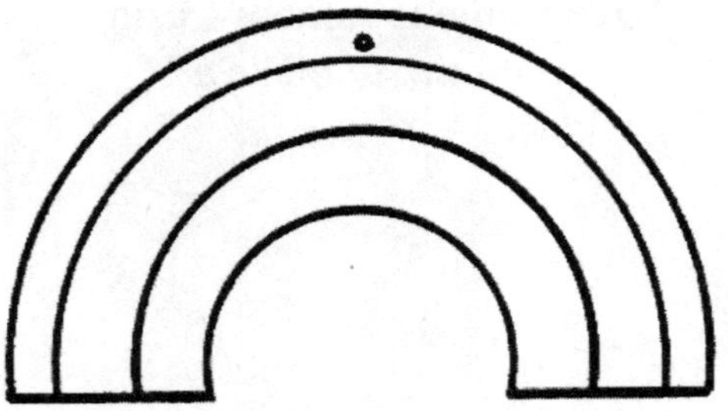

SIZE WHEN SHRUNK

GAMES

I need:

X-Acto® knife

ruler

carpet

scissors

jug lids

permanent marker

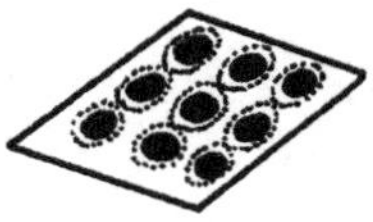

stickers

MATCHING

1 Put stickers inside the lids. Make sure you use the same sticker twice. Make as many as needed.

GAME MARKERS

2 Put stickers on outside of lid. Use only one of a kind.

CHECKERS

3 Use two different colored lids. You will need twelve of each color. Use short nap carpet remnant, at least 12" x 12". Measure 1 ½" x 1 ½" squares, sixty-four in total. Draw squares with permanent marker. Shade in every other square to make a checkerboard.

JANANNA TIPS

Game suggestions for game markers are Noah's Ark and Garden of Eden. I have provided patterns for these games.

SNAKE IN PATH
GO BACK
2 SPACES

HELPED A CAT
MOVE 1 SPACE

FALLEN APPLE
GO BACK
1 SPACE

START

NAMED ANIMALS
MOVE 2 SPACES

GARDEN OF EDEN

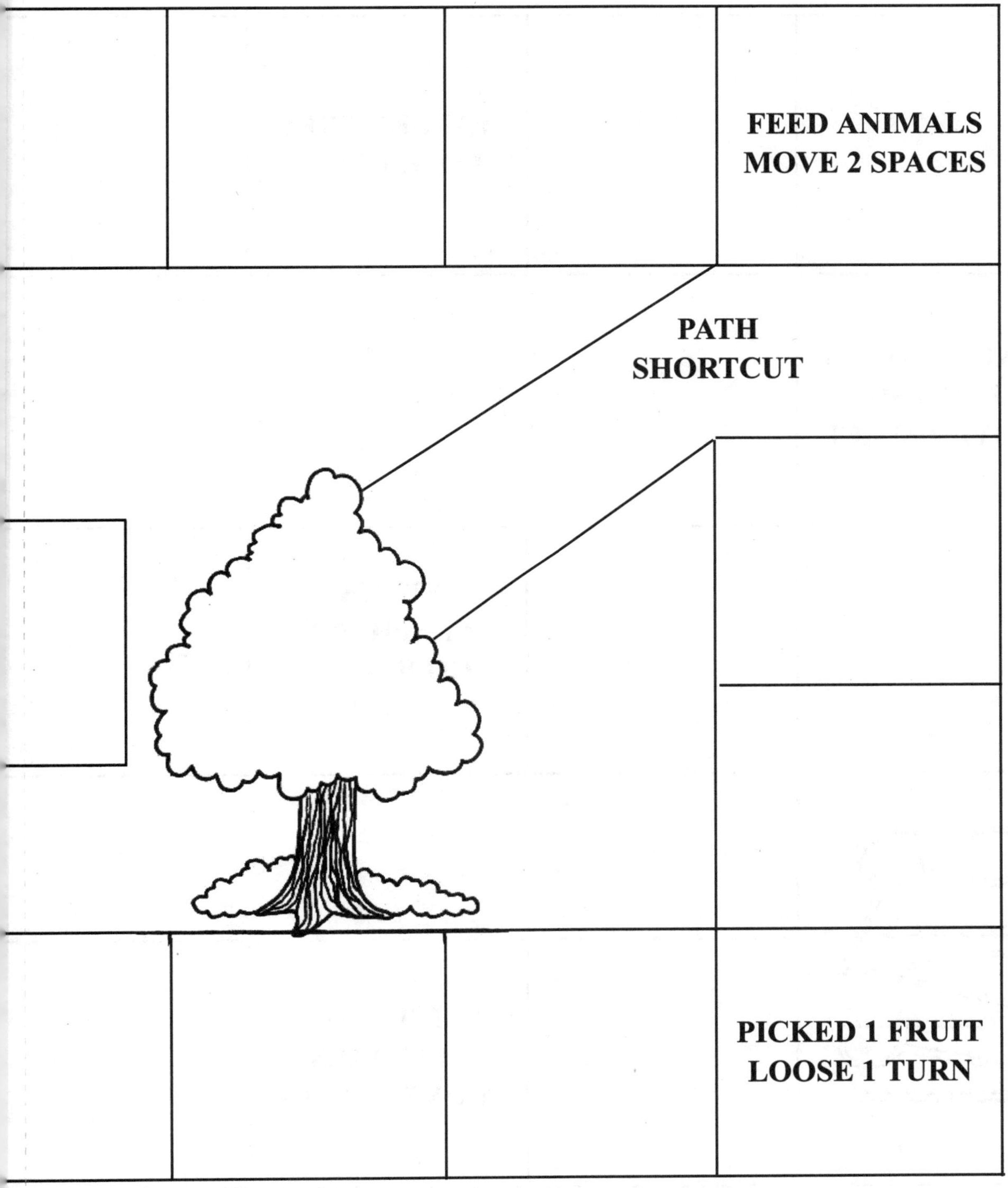

RULES: Roll dice to move. If you land on Path Shortcut, you may go directly to the Tree. Follow the instructions in special marked spaces. You must roll exact number to move into the Tree.

**FALLEN TREE
LOSE 1 TURN**

**RAIN CLOUDS
COMING
MOVE 1 SPACE**

**STUCK
ELEPHANT
GO BACK 1
SPACE**

START

**HELPING
ANIMALS
MOVE 1 SPACE**

NOAH'S ARK

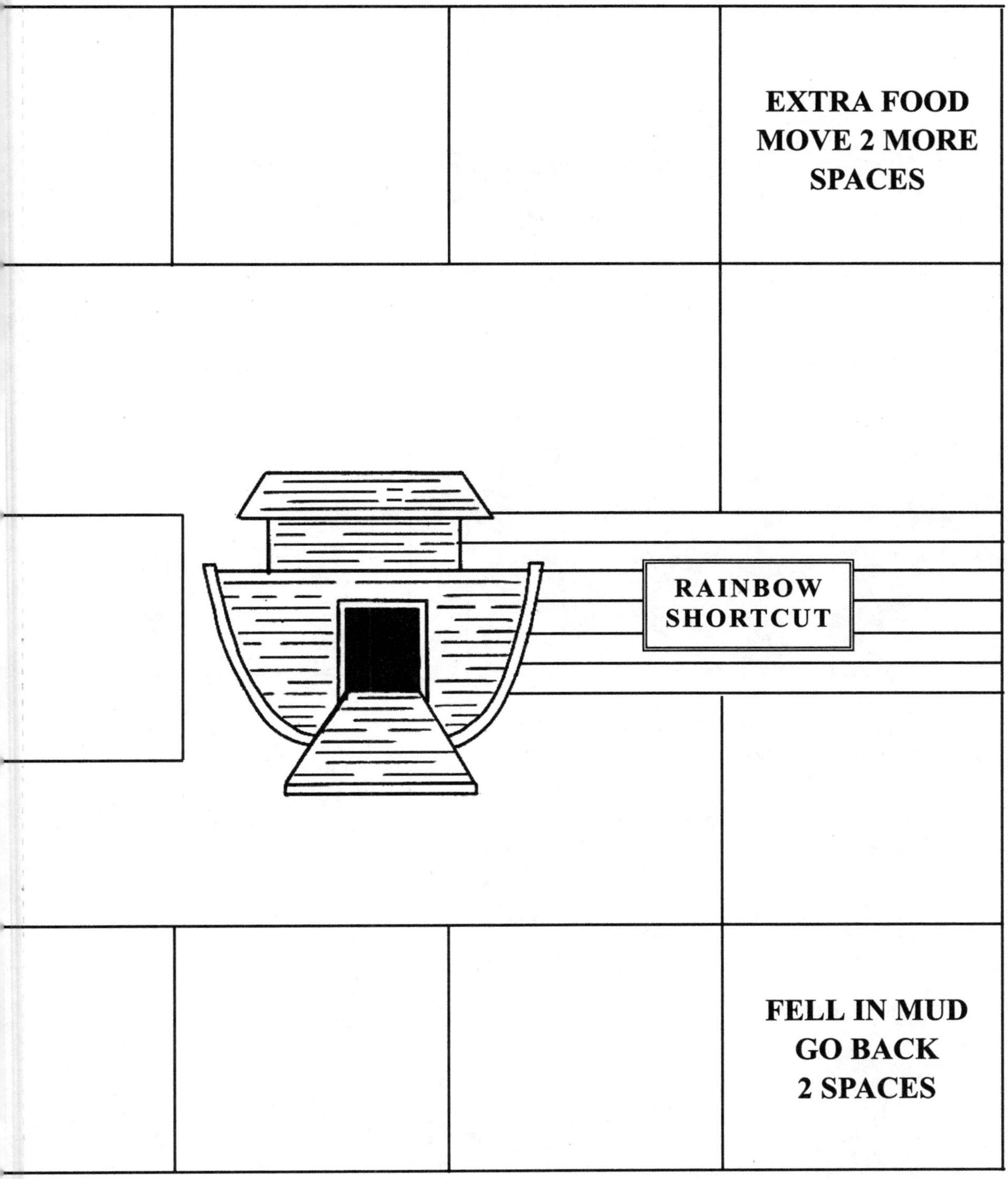

RULES: Roll dice to move. If you land on Rainbow Shortcut, you may go directly to the Ark. Follow the instructions in special marked spaces. You must roll exact number to move into the Ark.

LILAC FLOWER AND BASE

I need:

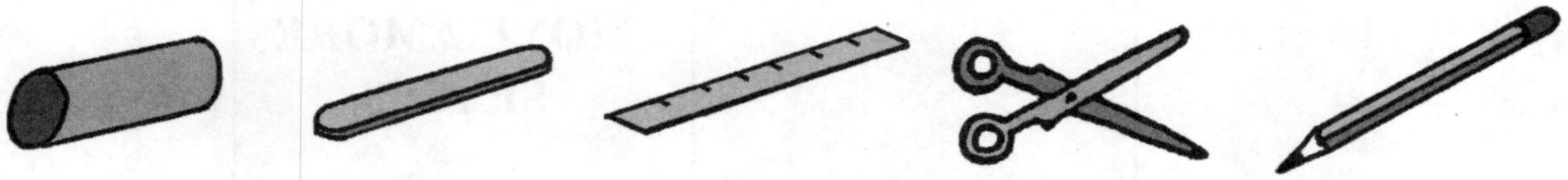

toilet paper roll | popsicle stick | ruler | scissors | pencil

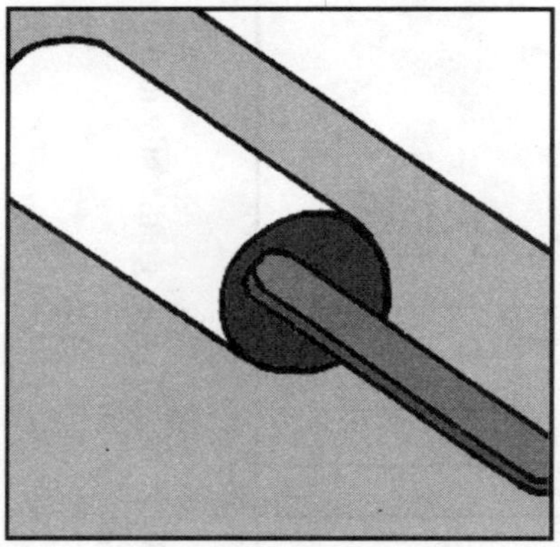

1 Glue 1" of a popsicle stick to the inside of a toilet paper roll and let dry.

2 Trace flower pattern and cut several squares of desired color of tissue paper.

3 Using the eraser end of a pencil, center the tissue square on the eraser end and press down, wrapping the paper around the eraser end.

white glue

yogurt cup
and lid

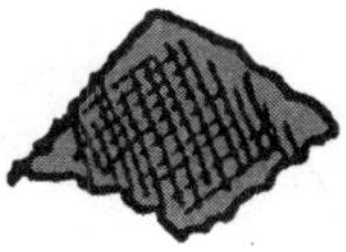

aluminum foil

tissue paper

4 With the tissue still on the pencil, dab the tissue end in glue. Then place the tissue end on the toilet paper roll. Continue steps three and four until the toilet paper roll is covered with tissue flowers. Let dry.

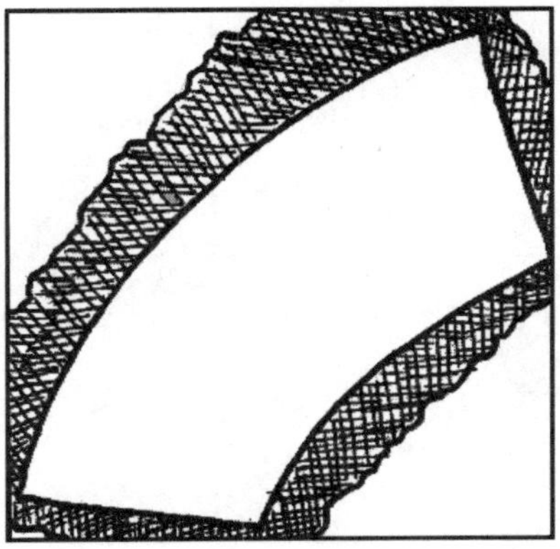

5 Trace the pattern for the base on used foil and cut out.

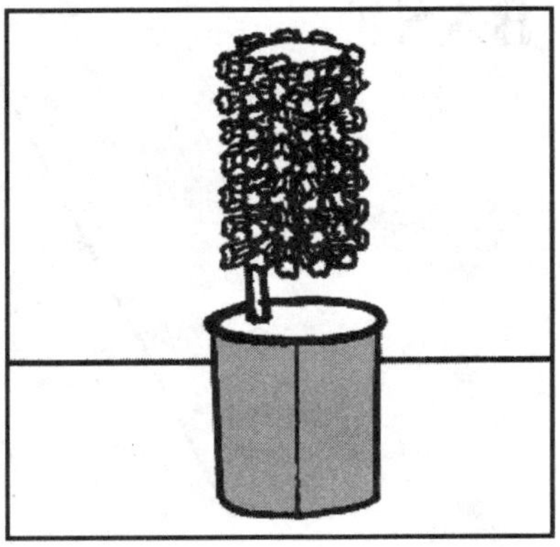

6 Wrap the foil around the cup. Then glue foil in place and let dry. Put lid on cup. Then cut a small slit off-centered on lid and put the popsicle stick in the slit. Glue stick in place and let dry.

JANANNA TIPS

Spray the tissue paper flowers with your favorite perfume. It will make the room smell great!

LILAC FLOWER AND BASE PATTERNS

BASE

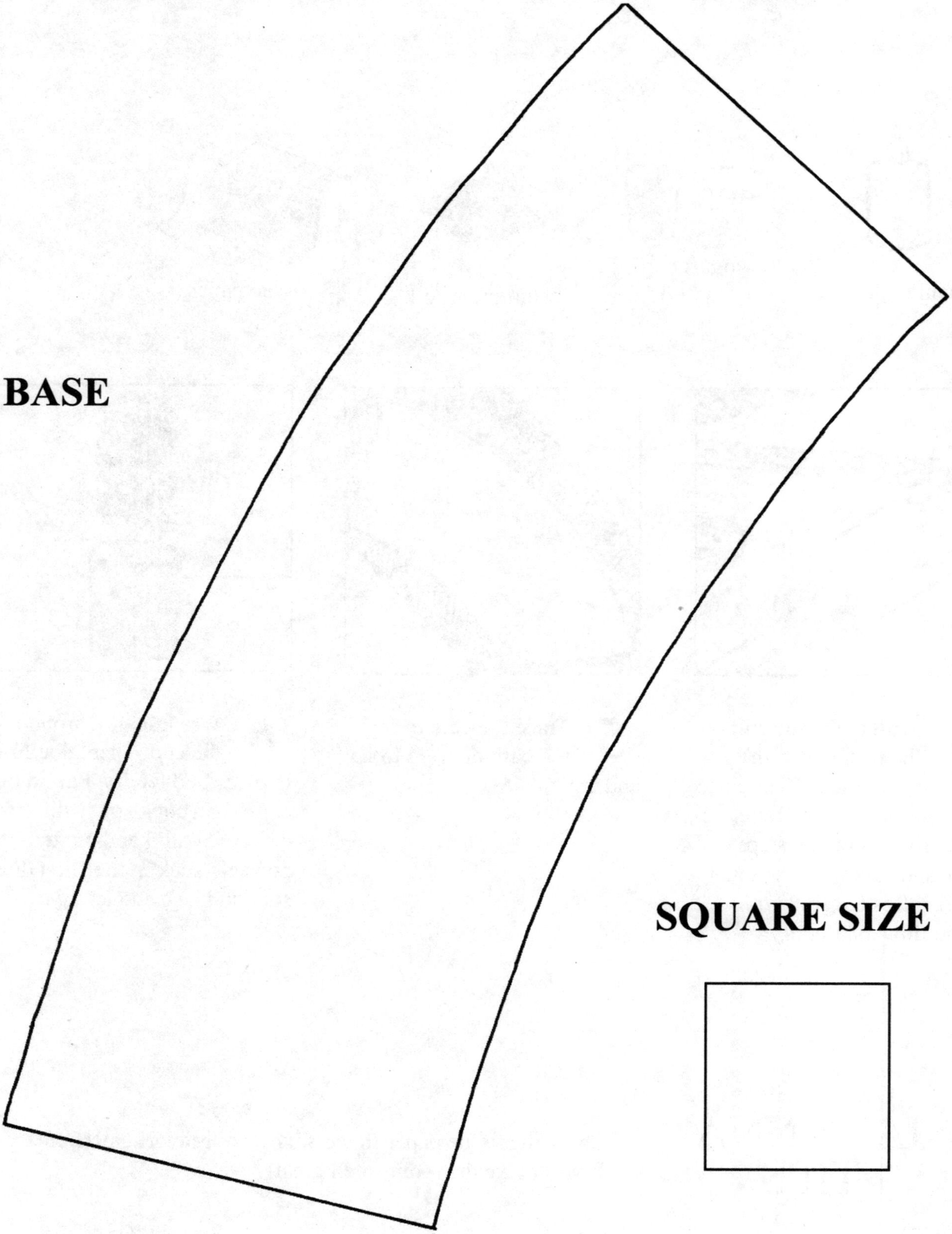

SQUARE SIZE

BEADS

I need:

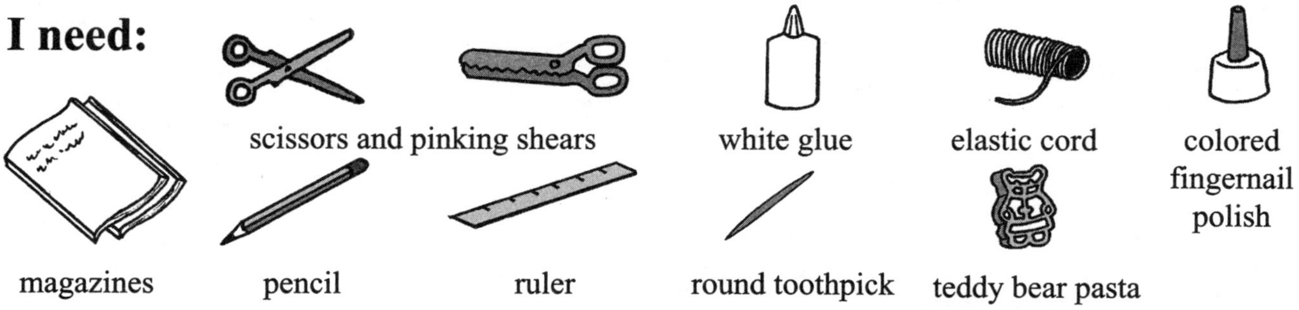

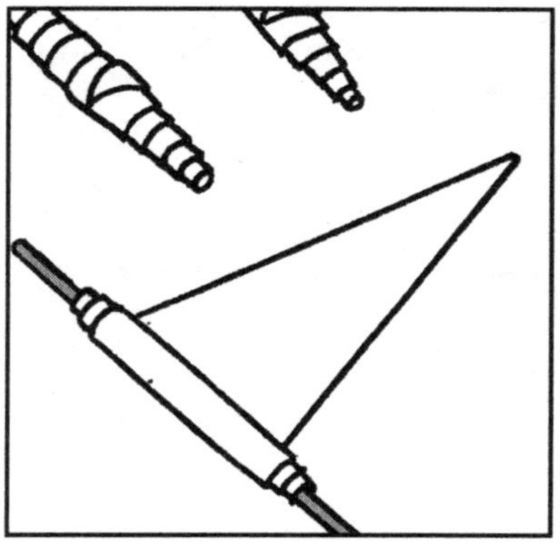

1 Trace and cut out desired amount of triangles and oval patterns from colorful magazine pages.

2 Starting with the wide end of paper, wrap the paper shape tightly around the toothpick. When the paper is completely wrapped, add a touch of glue to hold end of paper in place. Slowly slide the paper bead off the toothpick. Repeat this step for desired amount of beads.

3 Paint pasta with colored fingernail polish and let dry. Cut an 18" of elastic cord for necklace. Then string desired amount of beads and pasta onto the cord. Tie ends of cord to make necklace.

JANANNA TIPS

- Buttons, wooden or plastic beads, cut straws, or pasta may be used as well.
- Elastic cord can be found at your local craft stores.

BEADS PATTERNS

OVALS

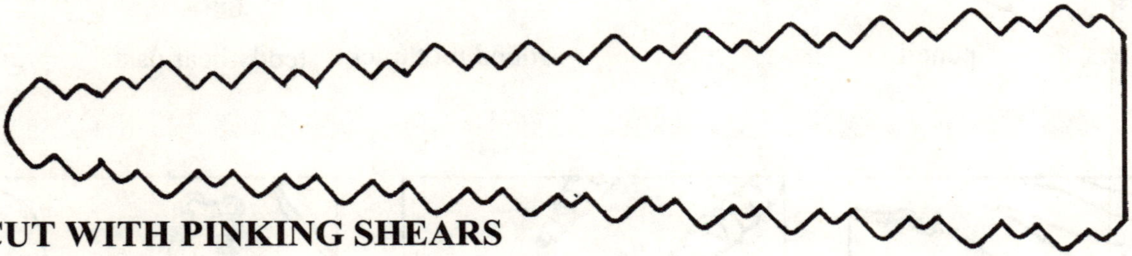

CUT WITH PINKING SHEARS

TRIANGLES

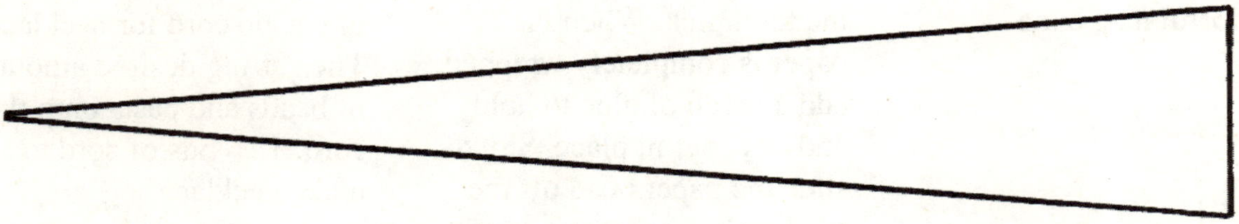

CUT WITH PINKING SHEARS

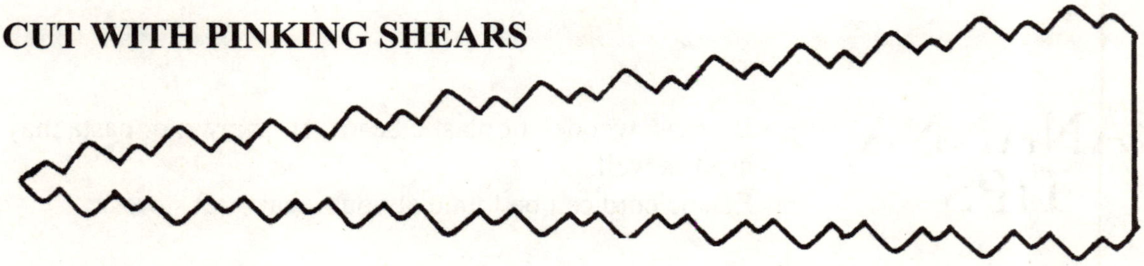

SAILBOAT

I need:

styrofoam meat tray | scissors | pencil | permanent marker | stickers

1 Trace pattern onto meat tray with a pencil.

2 Cut shapes out with scissors.

3 Put shapes together and decorate with markers and stickers.

JANANNA TIPS

Make paper doll figures on popsicle sticks and carefully poke into base to look like fishermen. Be sure to keep the boat balanced.

SAILBOAT PATTERNS

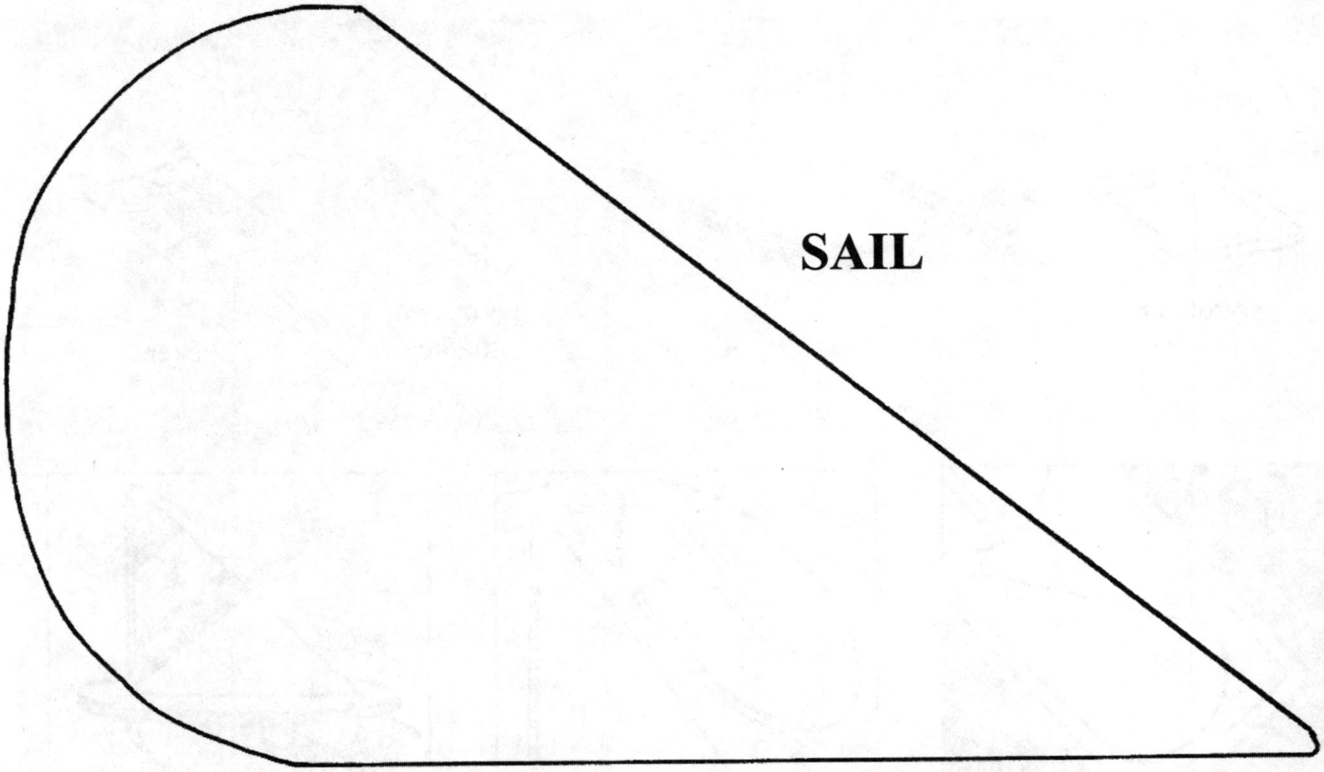

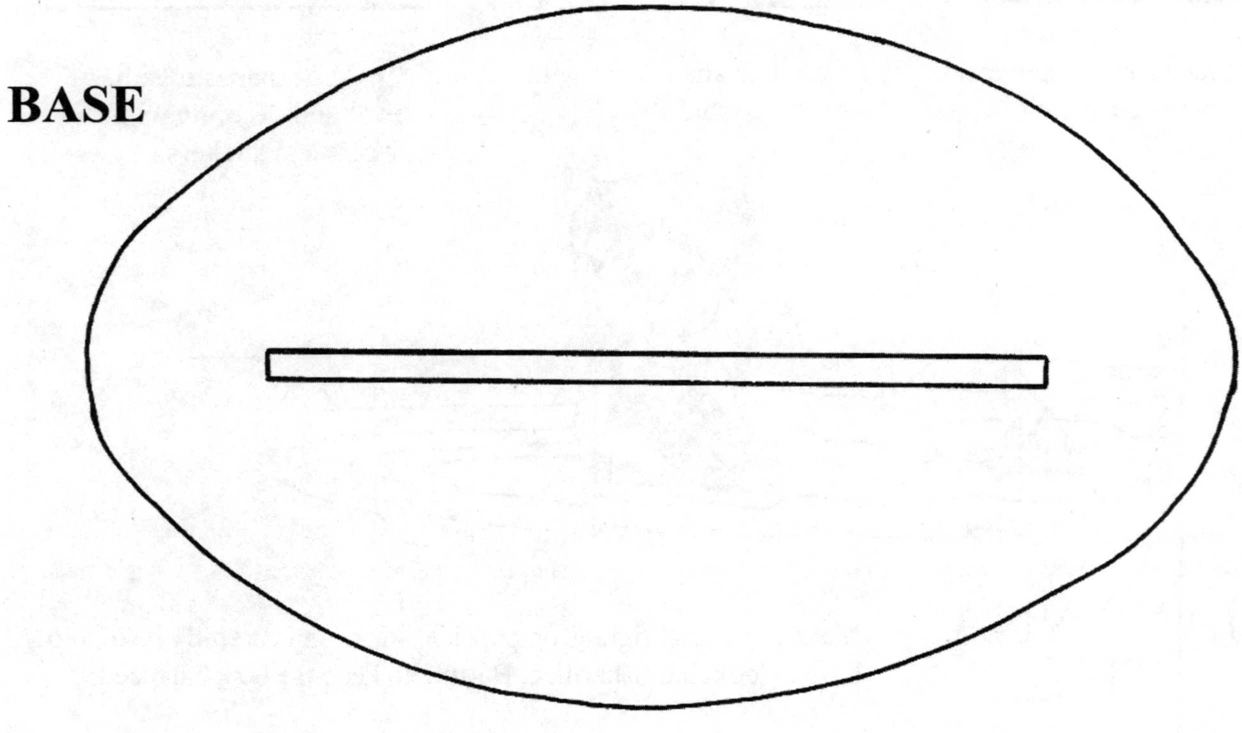

DOMINOES

I need:

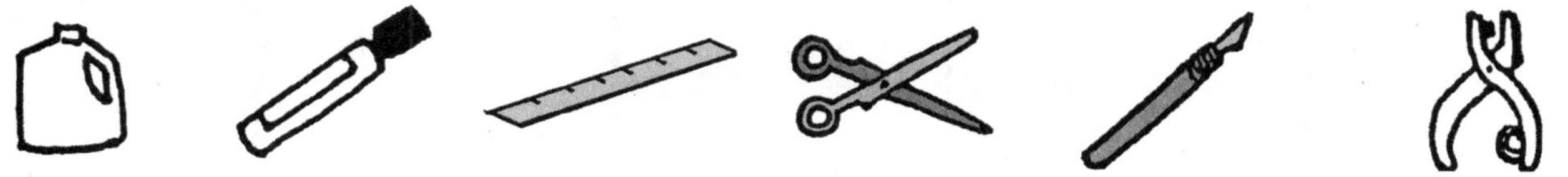

milk jug | permanent marker | ruler | scissors | X-Acto® knife | hole punch

1 Trace pattern with marker onto jug for desired number. Cut pieces out of jug.

2 Use ruler and marker to make divider bar on each piece. Punch desired amount of holes on each piece.

DOMINOES PATTERNS

FISH BOWL SHAKER BOTTLE

I need:

clear dish detergent bottle

scissors

paper clips

hot glue gun

colored laundry detergent bottles

hole punch

blue food coloring

wire cutters

permanent marker

1 Remove labels from bottle. Then trace pattern for fish on different colored laundry detergent bottles and cut out. Punch a hole in each fish. Then cut and glue a small piece of paper clip to tail for weight and let dry.

2 Soak fish in hot water for five minutes. Then bend the fish to fit through the mouth of the bottle. Fill bottle with blue-colored water by adding one drop of blue food coloring to the water.

3 Make a hook out of the paper clip. Then glue hook to inside of lid and let dry. Fasten lid tightly on bottle. Now try to catch the fish on the hook!

JANANNA TIPS

- Have some summer fun by filling bottle with water and squirting a friend!
- Have some winter fun by filling bottles with colored water and squirting designs in the snow!
- Different sequins may also be added to the water of the shaker bottle.

SHAKER BOTTLE FISH PATTERNS

BUCKET

I need:

liquid laundry detergent bottle

scissors

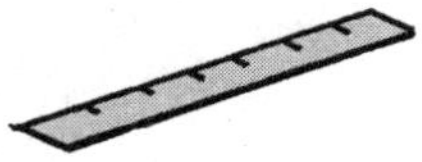

ruler

permanent marker

bread tie

hole punch

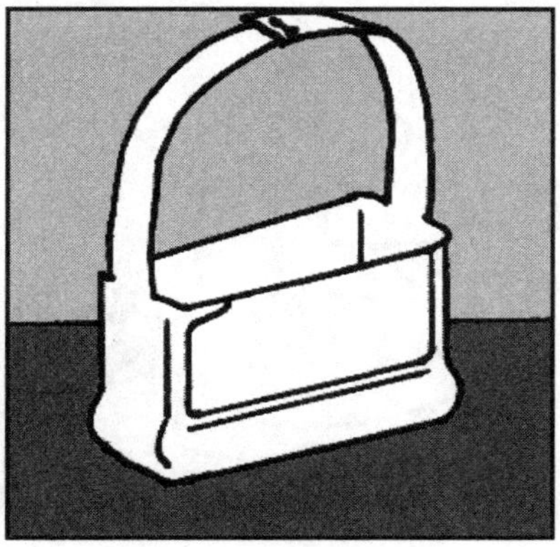

1 Remove labels from bottle.

2 Measure 4" from bottom of bottle. Cut from side to side on both sides of bottle. Make sure to leave a 1" space uncut to form the handles.

3 Measure and mark two 1" wide strips about 5" long for handles. Then cut out handles. Punch two holes at the end of each handle strip. Then tie handles together with a bread tie.

JANANNA TIPS

This makes a great Easter basket when decorated with lace, rickrack, and stickers.

CHURCH

I need:

milk jug

scissors

permanent markers

hot glue gun

green felt

X-Acto® knife

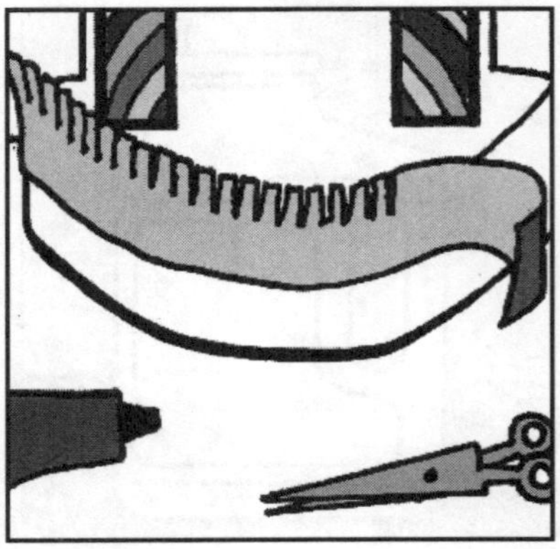

1 Trace pattern with marker onto jug. Also trace windows and flowers patterns on unused section of jug. With adult help, cut out form with knife or scissors. Spray paint entire jug with desired color and let dry.

2 Color or paint in windows with many colors to look like stained glass. Use markers or acrylic paints. Glue onto the church.

3 Cut 1" wide strip of green felt 12" long. Glue to dish part of jug with ½" of felt showing above edge. Cut top of felt to look like grass.

JANANNA TIPS

- Design for windows is only a suggestion. You may come up with your own ideas.
- Leaves for flowers may be made from felt or pipe cleaners.
- Cotton may be used instead of ½ " pom-poms.

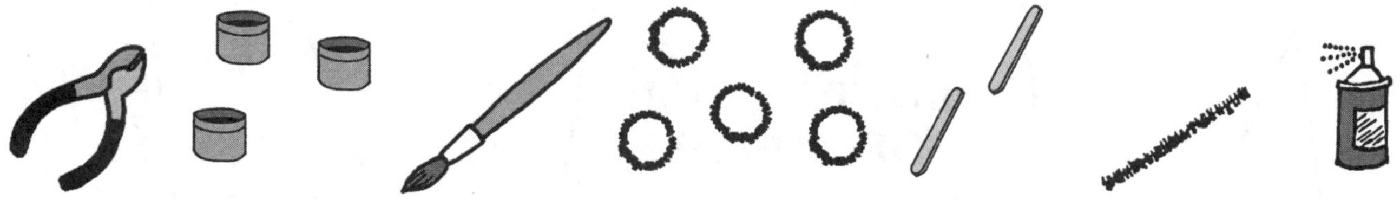

wire cutters | acrylic paints | paintbrush | several ½" pom-poms | two popsicle sticks | green pipe cleaners | spray paint

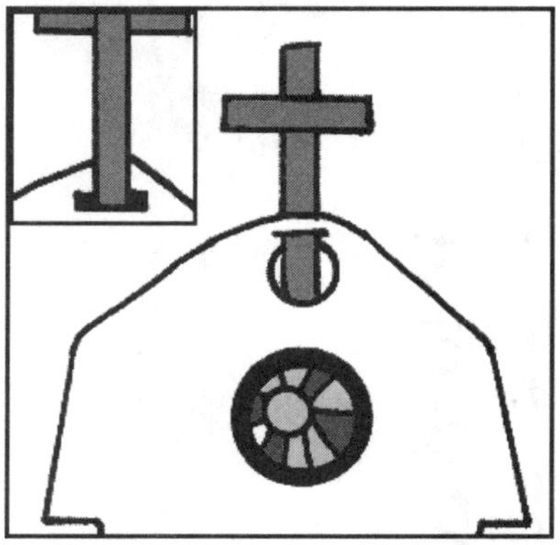

4 Paint flowers with spray paint or acrylic paint. Glue small ½" pom-poms for center of flowers and let dry. Cut 2" pieces of pipe cleaners for flower stems. Glue to backside of flowers.Then glue flowers to inside of dish.

5 Measure one stick at 4" and second stick at 2" to make cross. Glue together and let dry.

6 Cut slit in jug handle and place cross through slit. Glue in place.

CHURCH PATTERNS

CUT AWAY SECTION

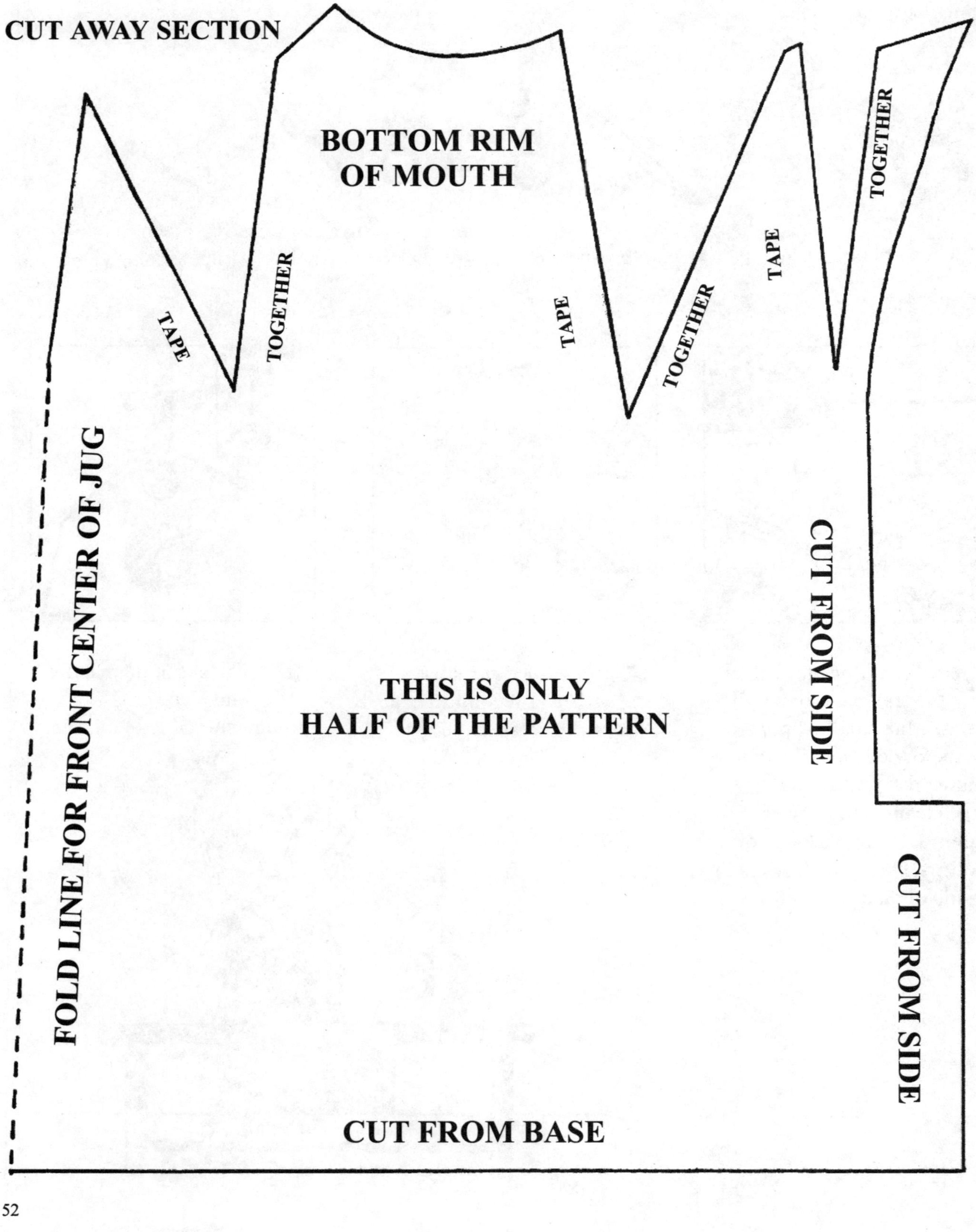

CHURCH PATTERNS

WINDOWS

FLOWERS

CAT

I need:

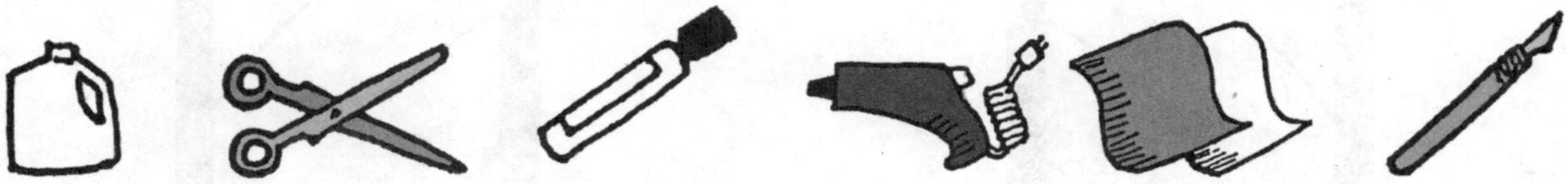

milk jug | scissors | permanent marker | hot glue gun | felt | X-Acto® knife

1 Trace pattern with marker. Cut out the one side of the jug.

2 Position mask on child's face. Mark eye and ear positions with marker.

3 Trace eye pattern with marker and cut out. For elastic ties, use hole punch at ear markings.

hole punch | pipe cleaner | spray paint | elastic cord | two 2" pom-poms | one ¾ " pom-pom

4 Trace ear pattern twice on unused section of jug and cut out. Spray paint ears and mask with desired color and let dry. Attach ears to mask with hot glue gun.

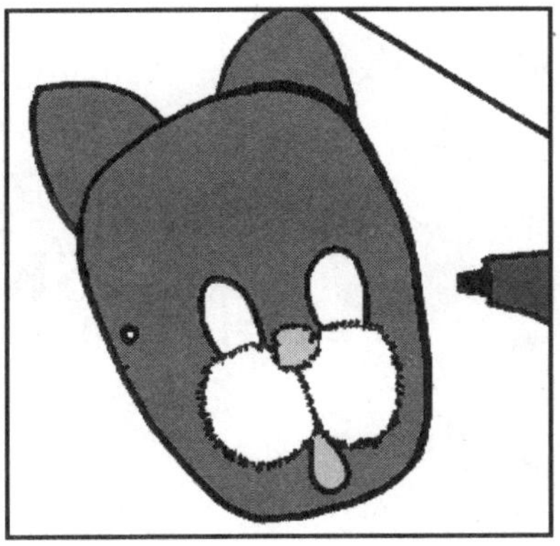

5 Glue large 2" pom-poms for cheeks. Glue ¾ " pom-pom for nose. Cut out felt tongue. Glue tongue onto the mask under 2" pom-poms.

6 Cut six 4" pieces from two pipe cleaners. Glue pieces into the large 2" pom-poms for whiskers. Cut two 12" lengths of elastic cord. Tie in ear holes.

JANANNA TIPS

- Cat may be changed to a lion by using felt teeth and yarn mane.
- Other suggestions for mane are fur, felt, or fringe.
- Tooth pattern is found with cat pattern.

CAT PATTERNS

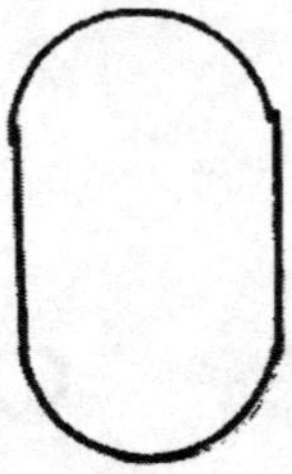

EYE
TRACE 2

LION TOOTH
TRACE 2

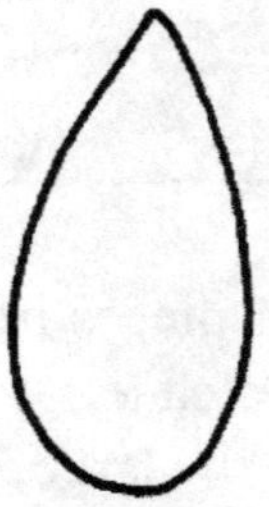

CAT TONGUE
TRACE 1

EAR
TRACE 2

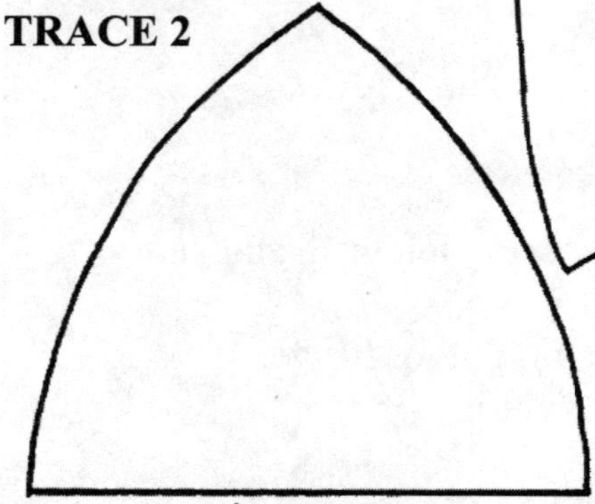

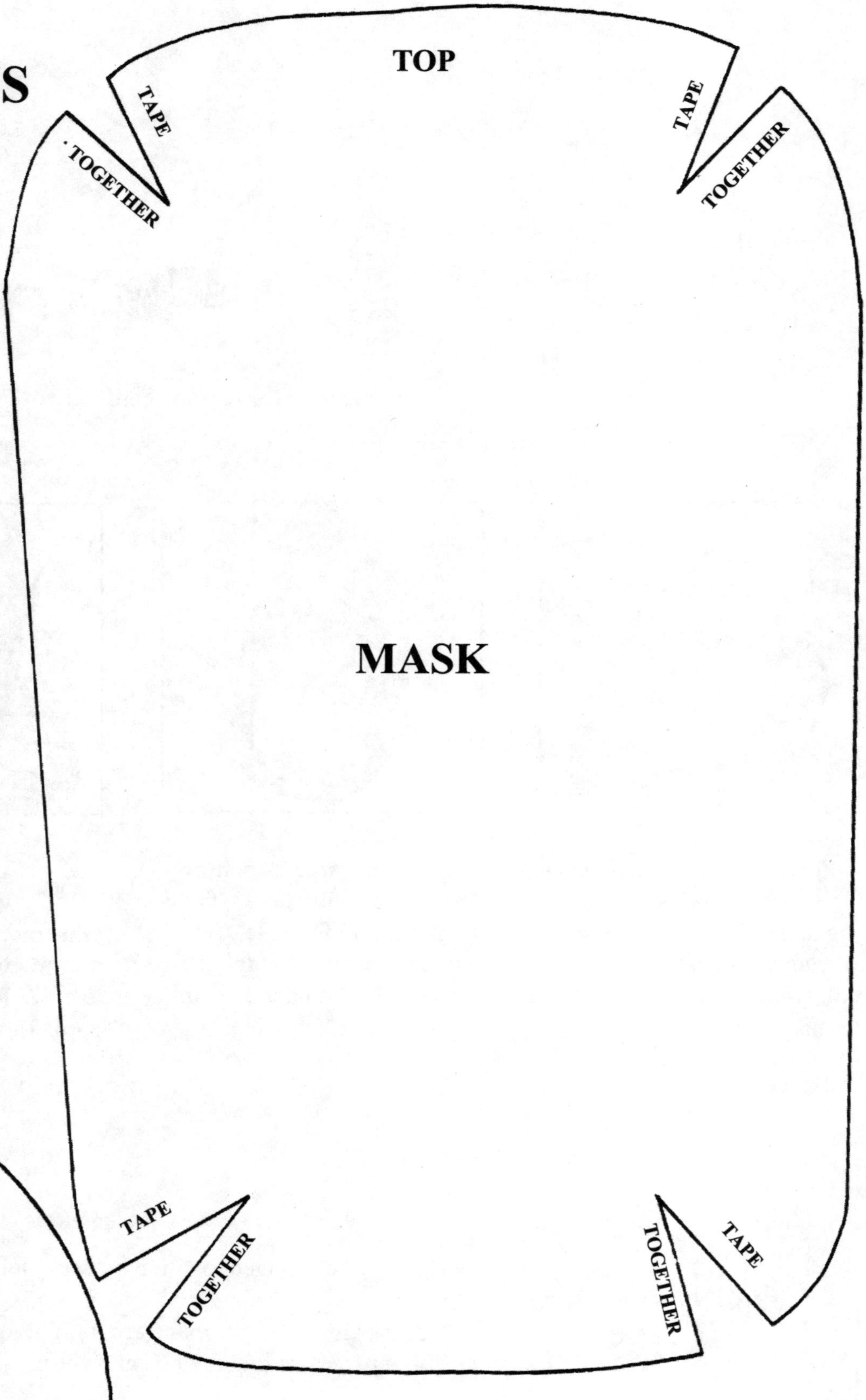

SIFTER

I need:

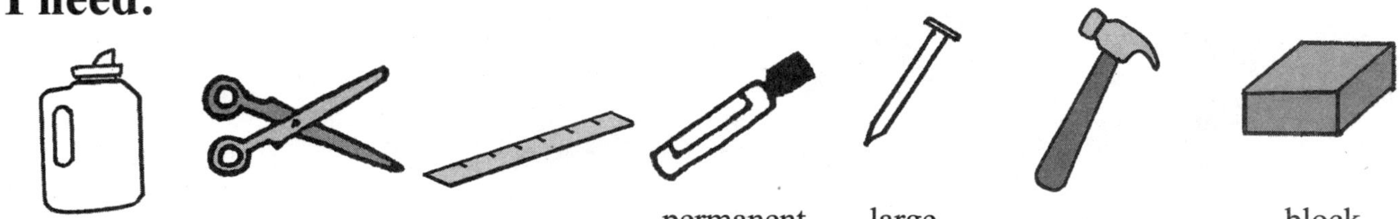

- liquid laundry detergent bottle
- scissors
- ruler
- permanent marker
- large nail
- hammer
- block of wood

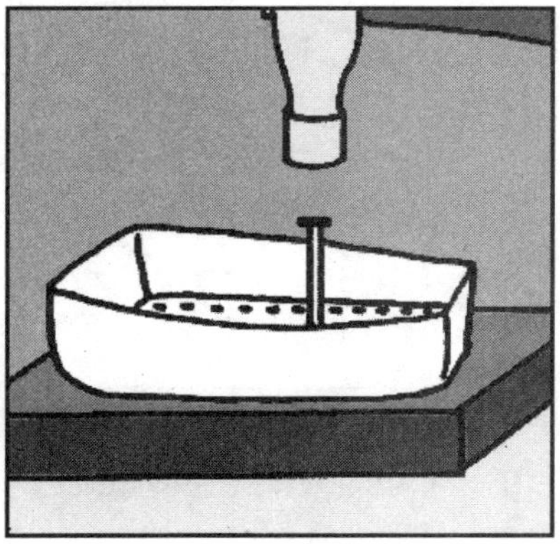

1 Remove labels from bottle.

2 Measure 3" from the bottom of the bottle. Then cut around the bottle, using the bottom as the sifter.

3 Place the bottom of the bottle on a piece of wood. Then hammer as many holes as desired with a large nail and a hammer.

JANANNA TIPS

An easier way to make holes is to have an adult use a drill and a desired size drill bit. Have an adult drill as many holes as desired.

LAMB

I need:

cardboard egg carton

X-Acto® knife

scissors

pipe cleaner

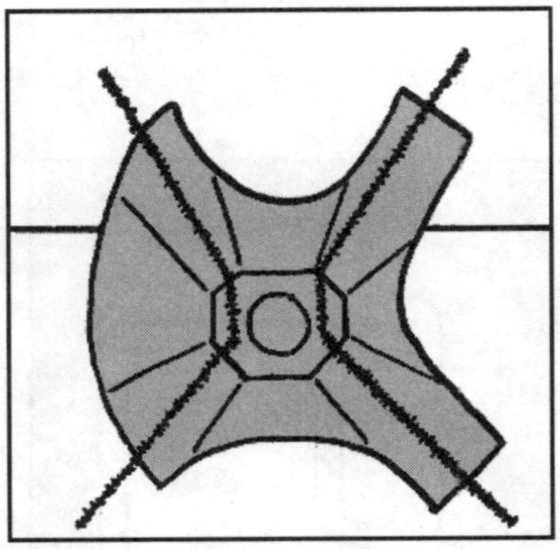

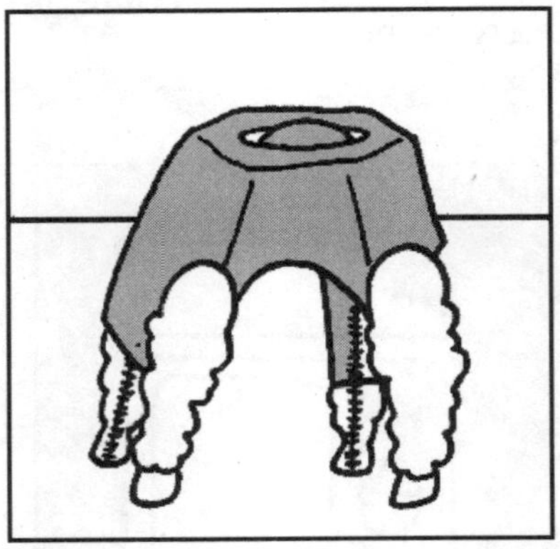

1 Cut out a single egg cup from the egg carton. Cut out head, legs, ears, and tail.

2 Cut a pipe cleaner in two 6" pieces and bend in a **U** shape. Glue both **U** shaped pipe cleaners inside the egg cup to form the legs. Let dry.

3 Attach leg pieces to pipe cleaners and egg cup and let dry.

JANANNA TIPS

Egg cartons can be used to hold markers. Turn egg carton upside down, and punch a hole in each cup large enough to hold a marker.

hot glue gun or white glue

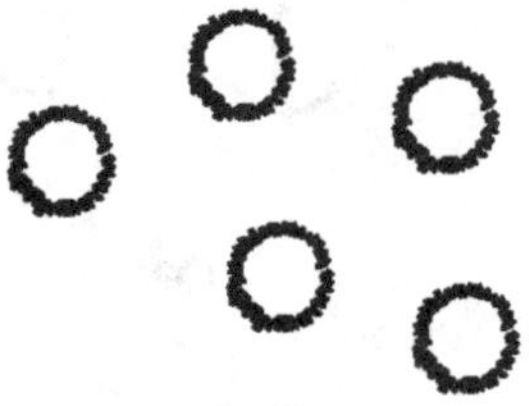

cotton balls

4 Fold head and glue together to the fold line. Bend folds out. Then glue folds to end of egg cup that is flat. Glue tail onto opposite end.

5 Glue ears to head on marked line.

6 Glue cotton onto part of head and legs. Then completely cover egg cup and tail with cotton. Glue cotton in place and let dry.

LAMB PATTERNS

EARS

TAIL

HEAD

LEGS

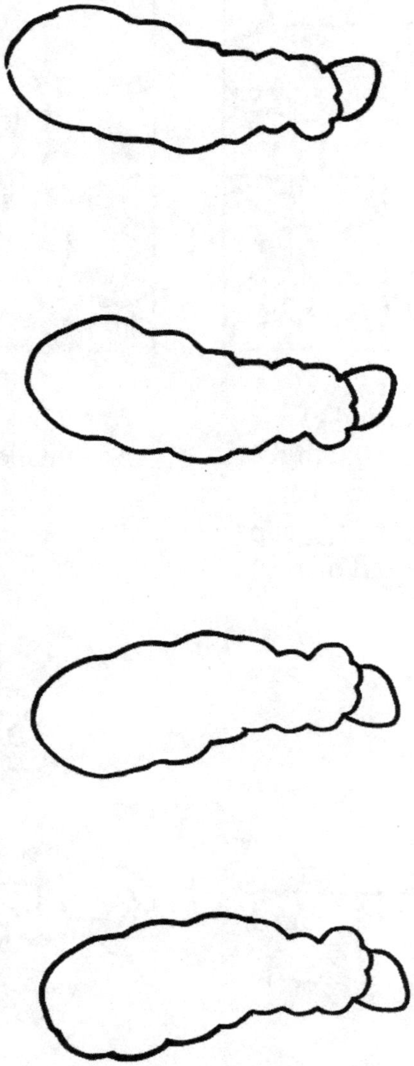

SCOOP

I need:

liquid laundry detergent bottle

scissors

permanent marker

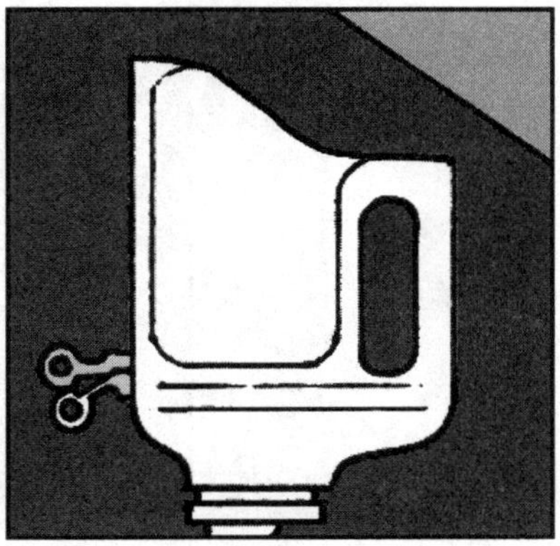

1 Remove labels from bottle.

2 Trace pattern on bottle.

3 Cut on line to make your scoop.

JANANNA TIPS	Save the lid to close the scoop. The lid can also be used for scooping!

SCOOP PATTERN

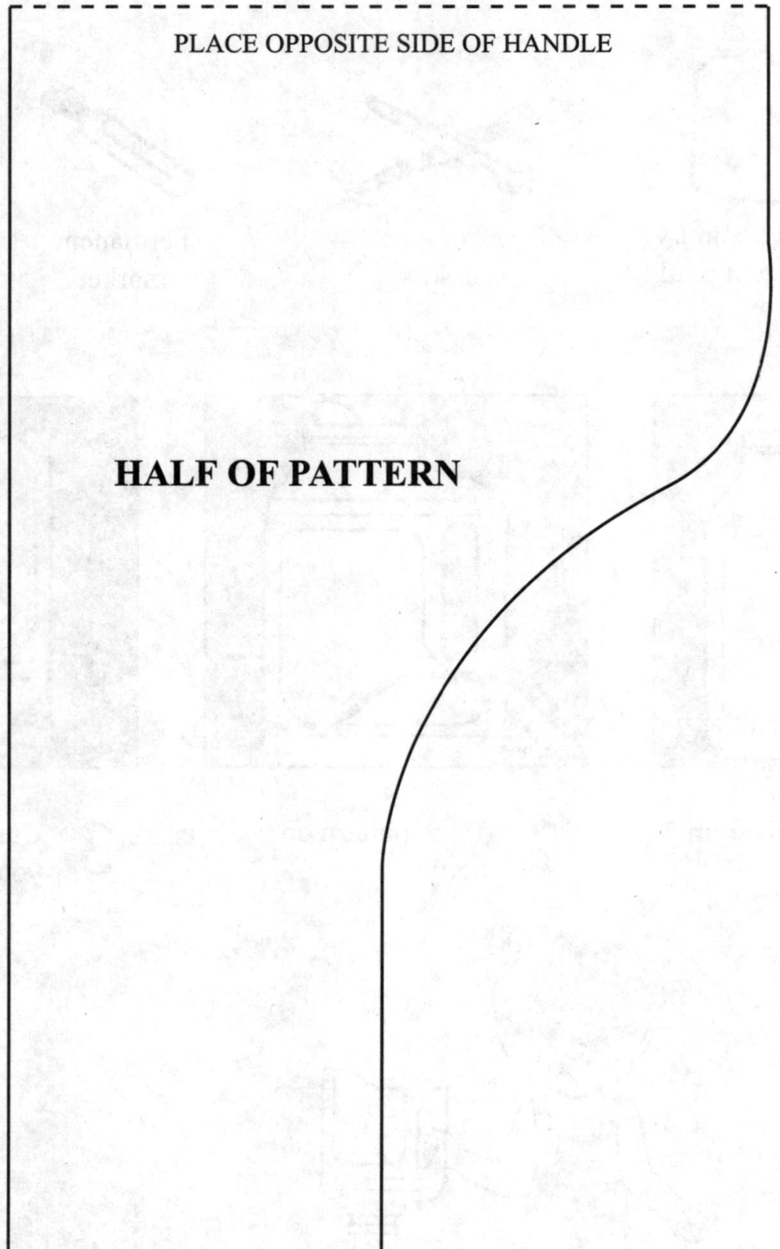

SNOW JAR

I need:

baby food jar, distilled water, hot glue gun, plastic figure, scissors, glitter, ¼" wide rickrack

1 Turn lid upside down and glue desired figure onto it. Let dry.

2 Put ½ teaspoon of glitter into jar. Fill jar just below the rim with distilled water.

3 Screw lid on jar tightly and glue together. Then glue one 7 ½" piece of rickrack around side of lid to decorate. Let dry.

JANANNA TIPS

- If you are afraid of the jar breaking, use a plastic peanut butter jar. If you are using a larger jar, you will need a teaspoon of glitter.
- I like to add a small amount of food coloring to the water, too.

ANGEL

I need:

milk jug

scissors

permanent marker

hot glue gun

ribbon

spray paint

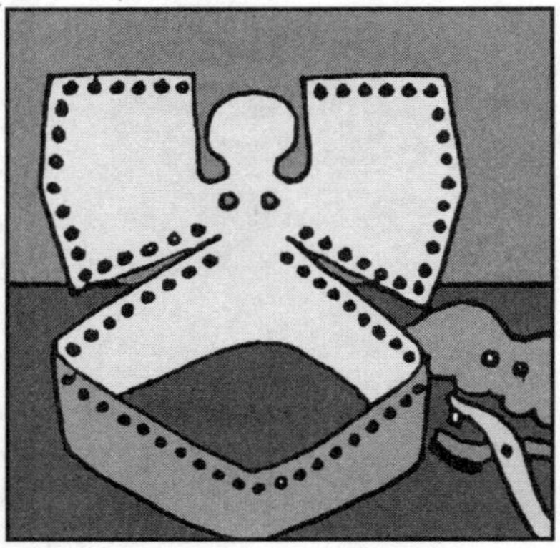

1 Trace pattern with marker onto jug. Head is drawn on opposite side from handle. Wings are traced behind handle. Cut out form with knife or scissors. Ask for adult help.

2 Punch holes at top and bottom of sleeve edges. Also punch holes on skirt edge, dish opening, wings, and neck. Spray paint entire body of angel with desired color. Let dry.

3 Glue flesh-colored felt on head. Use marker to draw chin line. Glue craft eyes onto face. Use markers for eyelashes and mouth. Make halo from pipe cleaner and glue onto back of head. Cut out front and back hair and glue on form.

JANANNA TIPS

Curling ribbon can be used instead of felt for hair.

5mm eyes | felt | X-Acto® knife | foil | hole punch | pipe cleaner

4 Match top and bottom holes on sleeves and lace together to make a cylinder shape. Finish angel by lacing remaining holes.

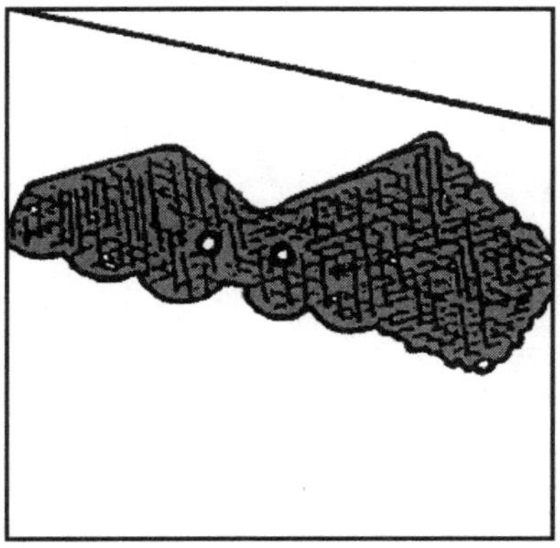

5 Cover wings with 12" of used foil. Make sure the front and back of wings are completely covered, except the two holes. Glue loose edges if necessary.

6 Cut 8" of ribbon and lace through holes on wings. Then lace through holes at neck of angel and tie in a bow in front.

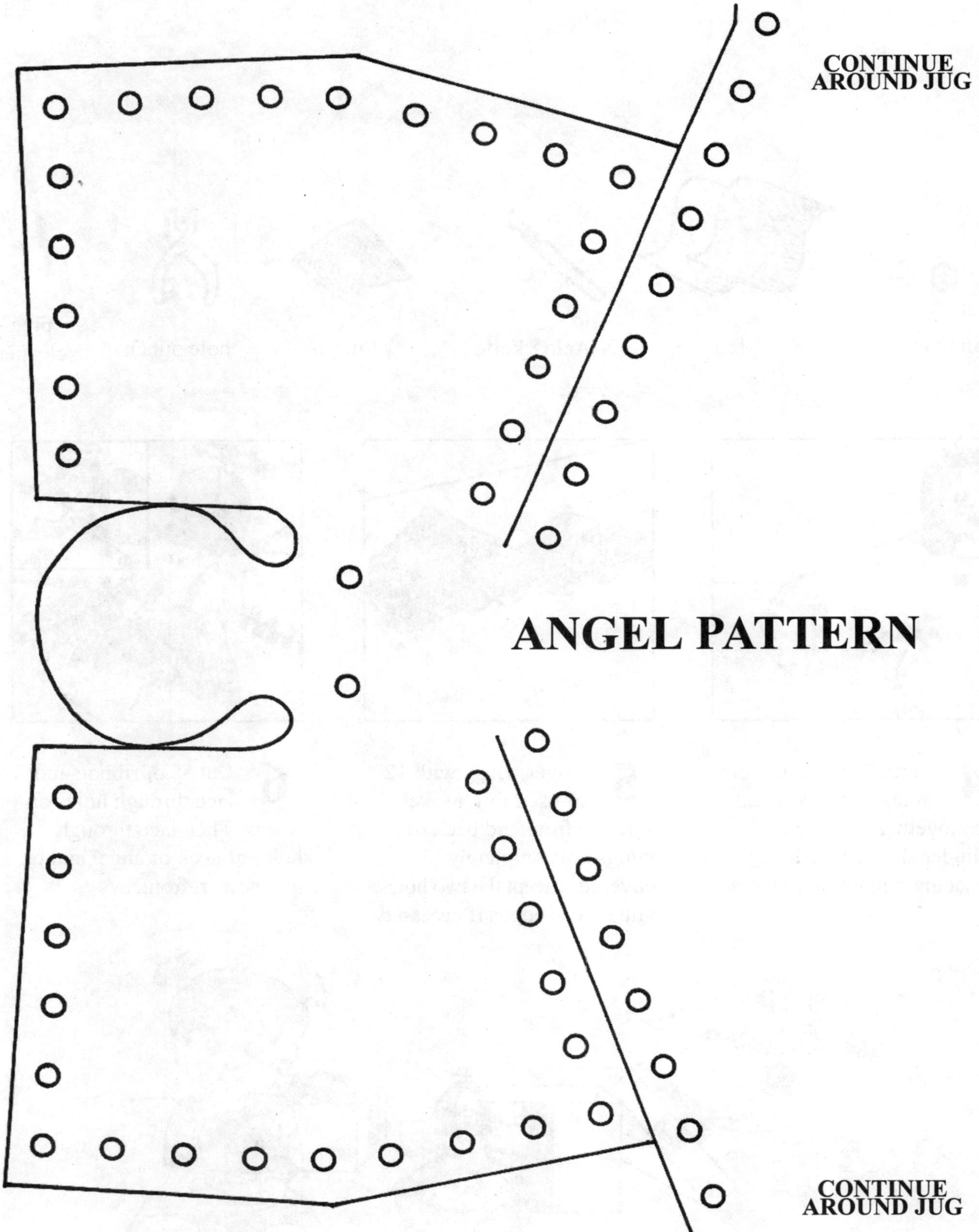
CONTINUE
AROUND JUG
ANGEL PATTERN
CONTINUE
AROUND JUG

ANGEL PATTERNS

WINGS

FACE

HAIR FRONT

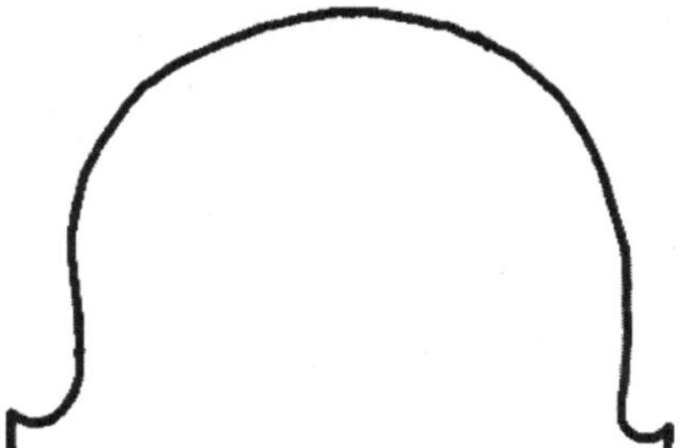

HAIR BACK

CHRISTMAS SCENE CANDLEHOLDER

I need:

white glue

decorations

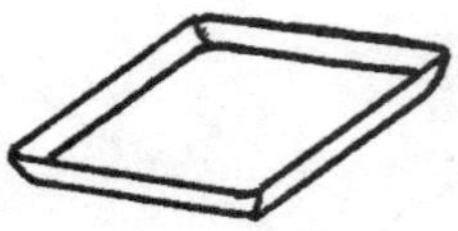

styrofoam meat tray

scissors or X-Acto® knife

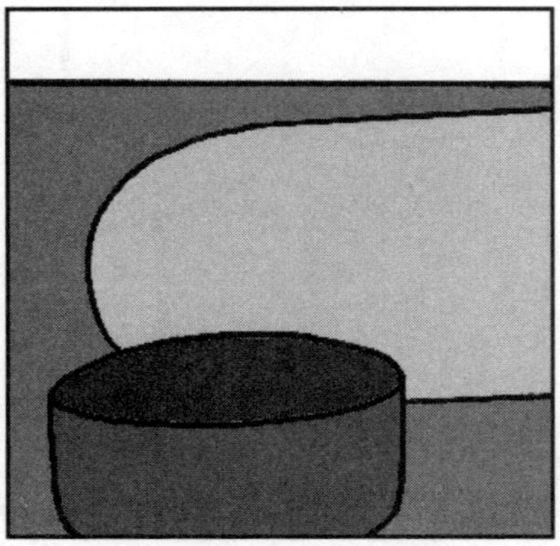

1 Soak bottle base in hot water for three to five minutes. Then pull base off of bottle carefully. Ask for adult help.

2 Cut top off of bottle about six inches down with scissors or knife. Ask for adult help.

3 Turn base upside down and trace outline onto a styrofoam meat tray. Cut out shape with scissors. Then glue styrofoam shape into base and let dry. **CAUTION: Hot glue will melt the styrofoam, so use white glue.**

JANANNA TIPS

- In step three, by not gluing the styrofoam shape into the base, you can change the decorations.
- In steps five and six, if candle is not desired, use dome shape of bottle for the cover.

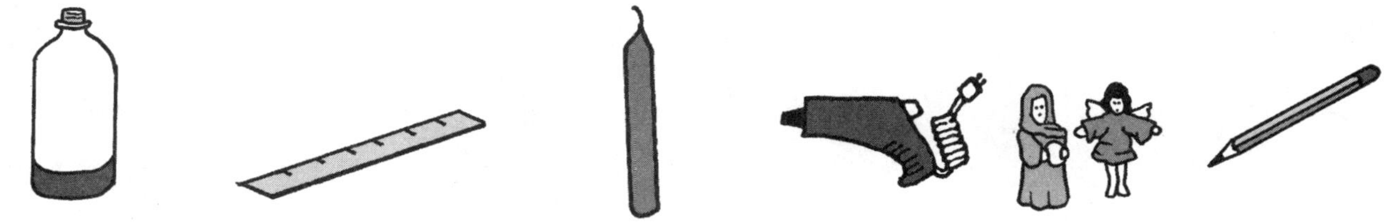

2-liter pop bottle | ruler | candle | hot glue gun | plastic figures | pencil

4 Choose plastic fugures to decorate the inside of the base. Then glue figures to inside of base with white glue and let dry.

5 Fit top of bottle inside of base to make a cover. **Optional:** glue top to base.

6 Decorate outside of base and mouth of bottle with holly, berries, and bows as desired. Glue candle inside the mouth of the bottle.

GREETING CARD COOKIE BOX

I need:

greeting cards

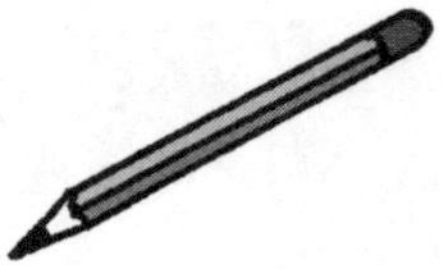

pencil

scissors

glue

1 Trace patterns on desired cards and then cut out.

2 Punch holes where shown on pattern.

3 Fold in edges on cards. Then glue sides, bottom, and top together and let dry.

JANANNA TIPS

- The box can be used instead of gift-wrapped boxes. Bread ties can be used instead of ribbon.
- Postcards can be made out of used cards for birthdays and Christmas.
- Stamp the word "Postcard," with a rubber stamp, onto the back of the used card.

POSTCARD

hole punch

ribbon

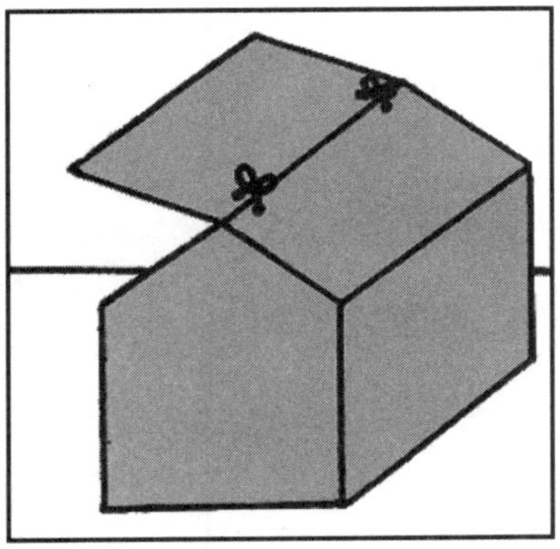

4 Glue flap to top piece and let dry. Then put ribbon through holes and tie in bows to form flap top.

5 Fill box with favorite cookies.

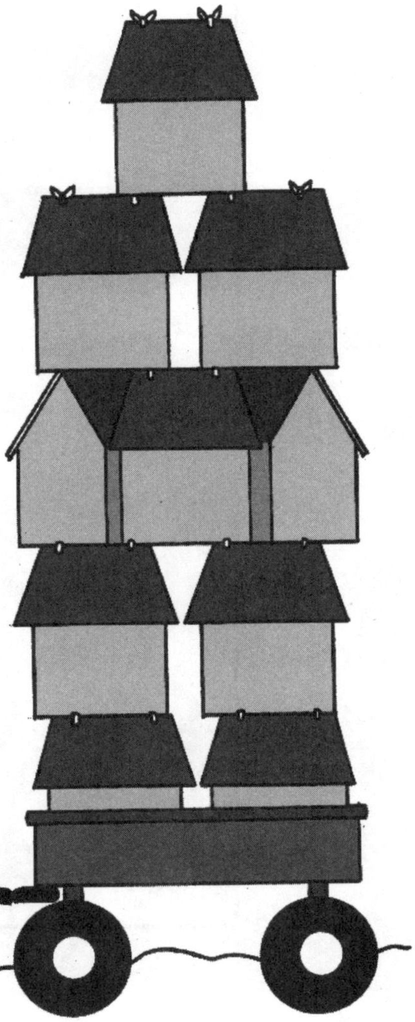

GREETING CARD COOKIE BOX PATTERNS

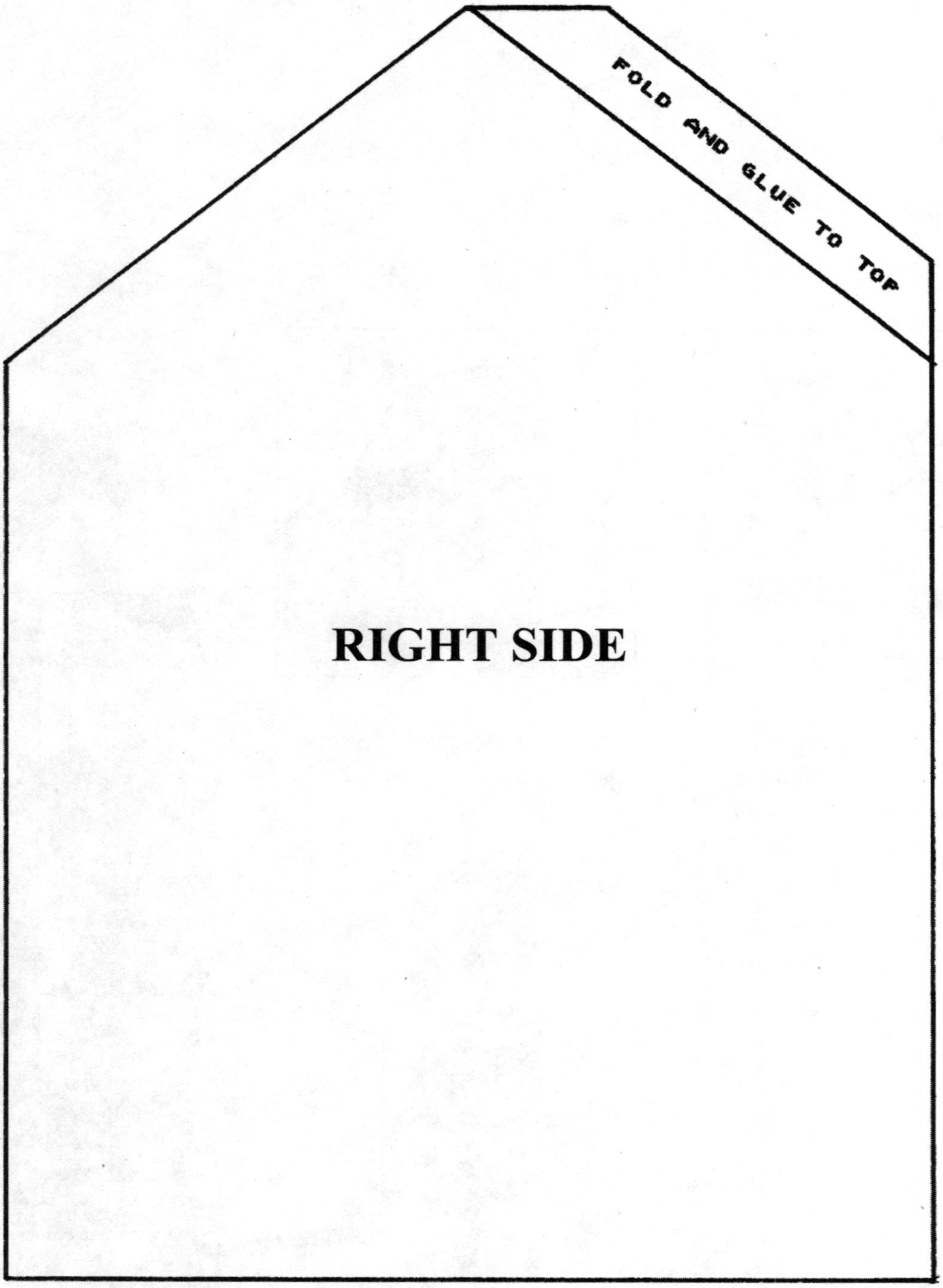

GREETING CARD
COOKIE BOX PATTERNS

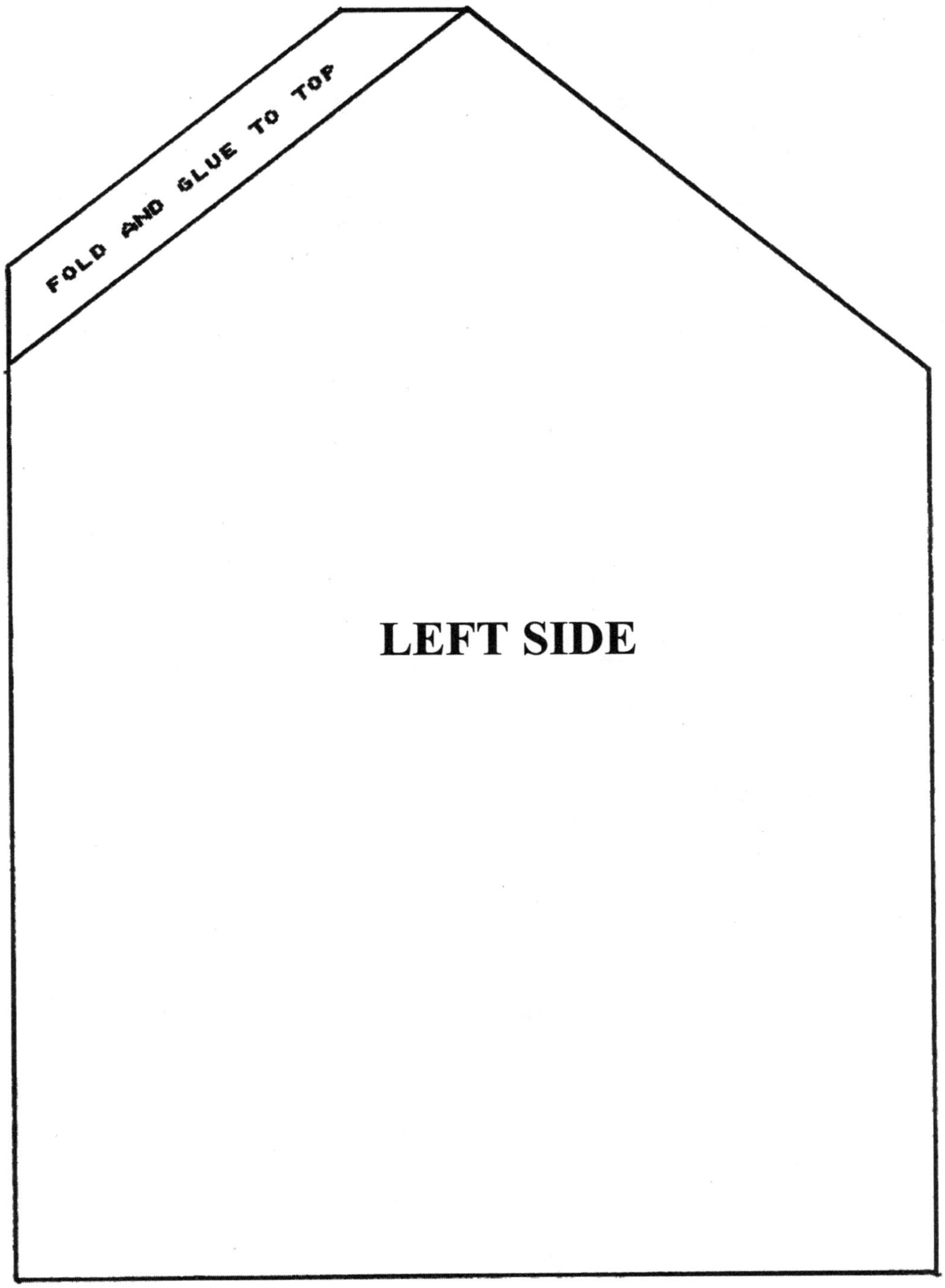

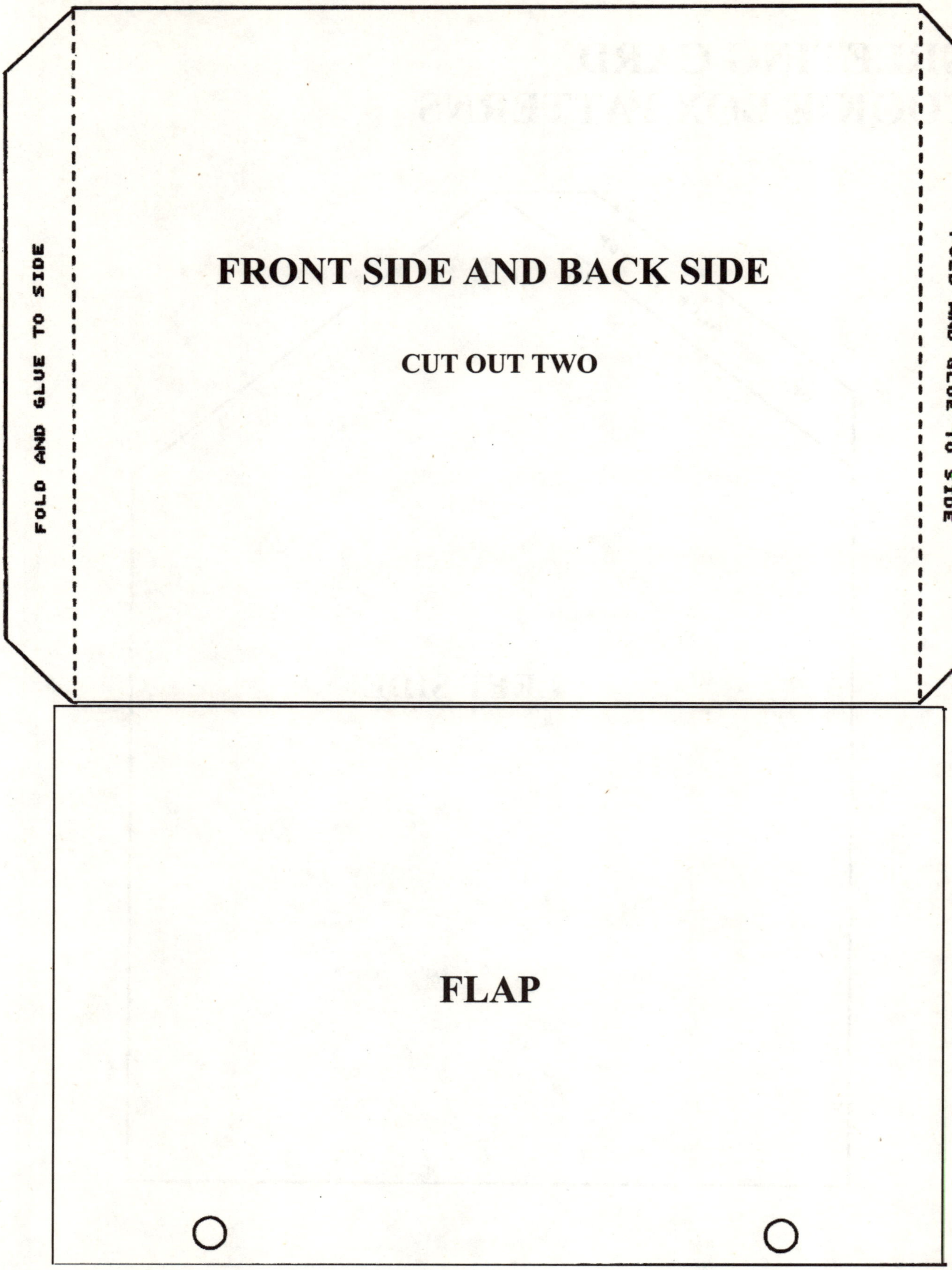
FRONT SIDE AND BACK SIDE
CUT OUT TWO
FOLD AND GLUE TO SIDE
FOLD AND GLUE TO SIDE
FLAP

GREETING CARD COOKIE BOX PATTERNS

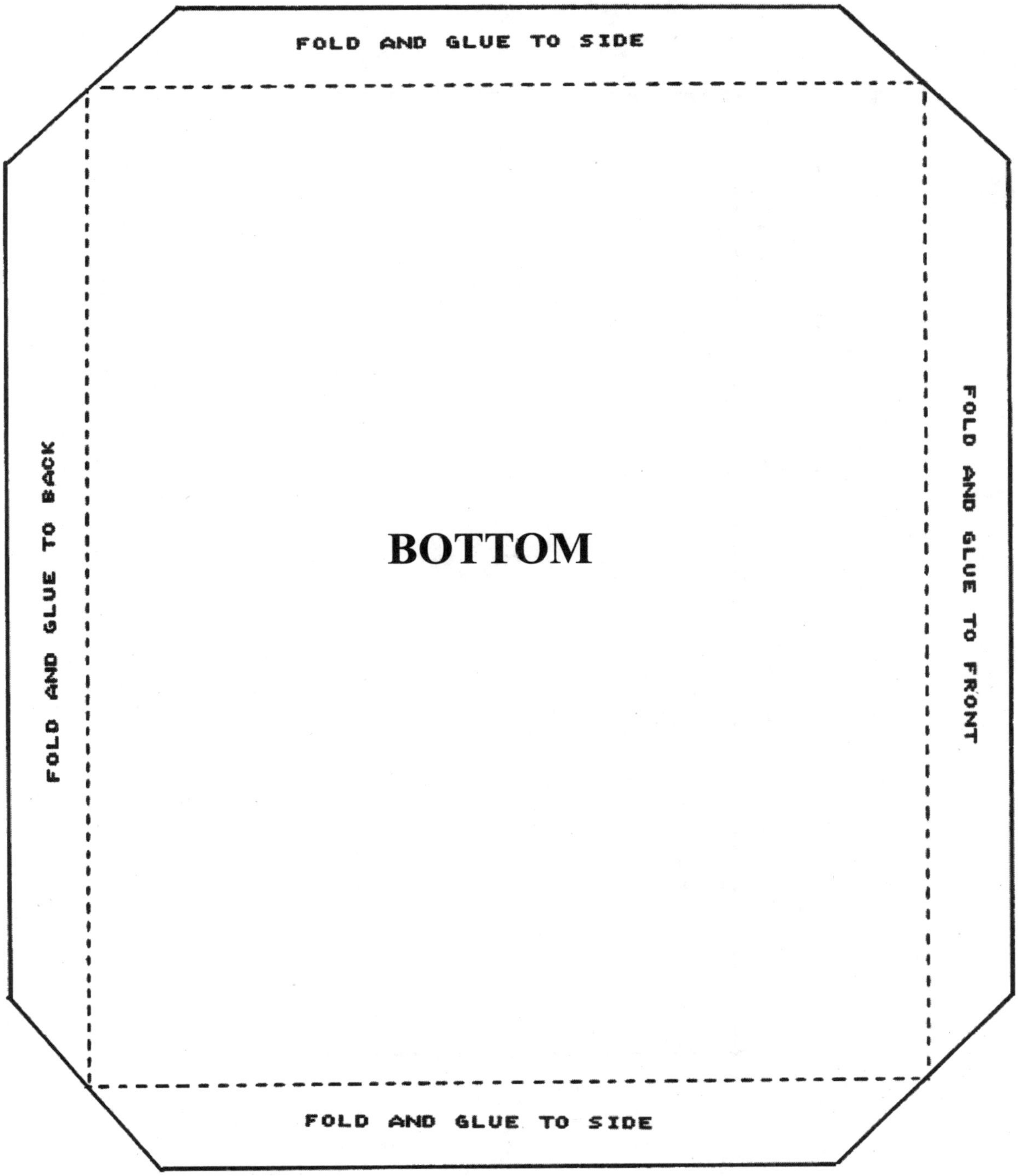

GREETING CARD COOKIE BOX PATTERNS

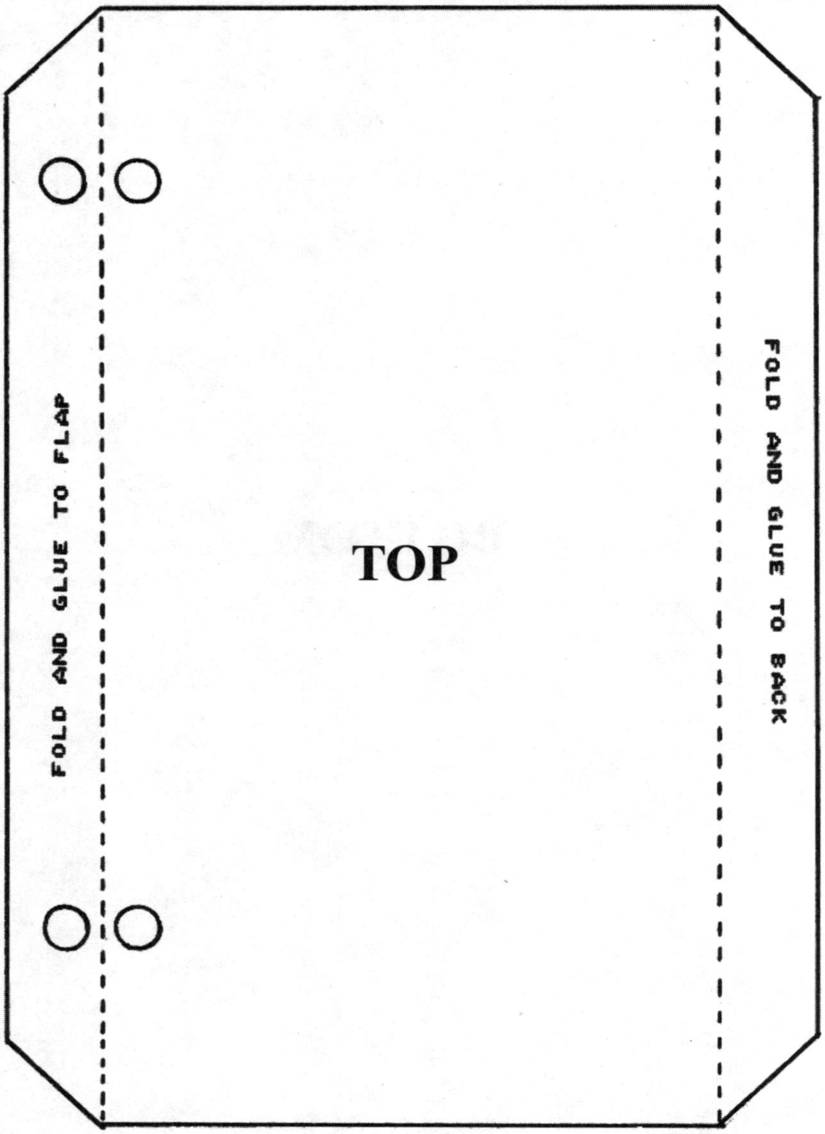

WREATH CANISTER

I need:

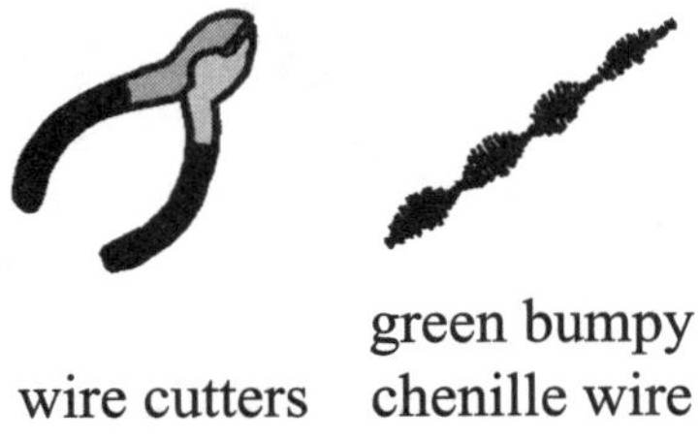

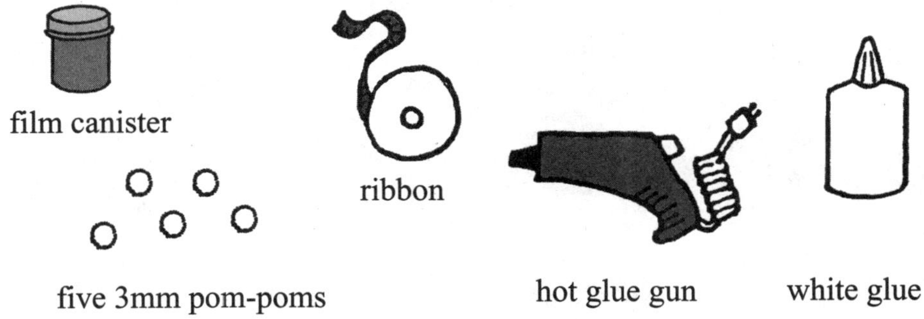

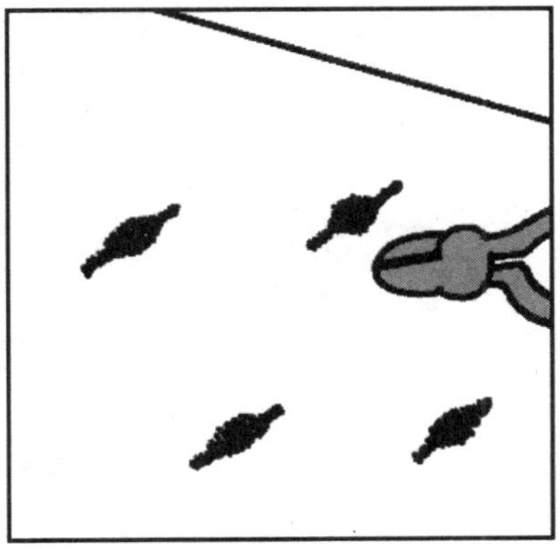

1 Cut a chenille wire in fourths.

2 Using two pieces, twist ends together to form a circle. Then glue circle to lid.

3 Glue pom-poms and bow to wreath and let dry. Then fill canister with candy or small nicknacks.

JANANNA TIPS

These are great stocking stuffers or to use at kids' school parties.

CAMEL

I need:

cardboard egg carton

brown spray paint

white glue

scissors

X-Acto® knife

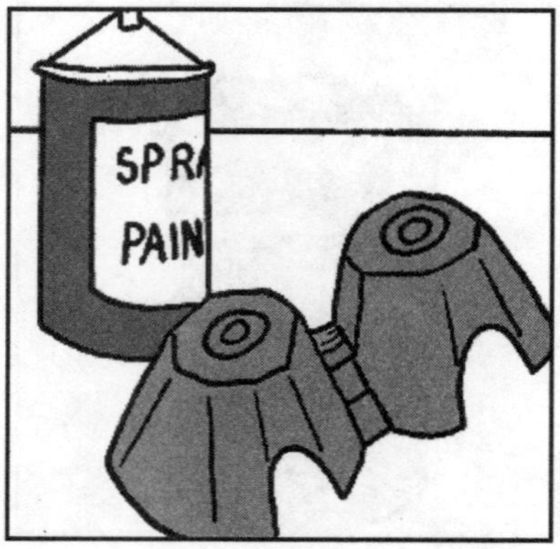

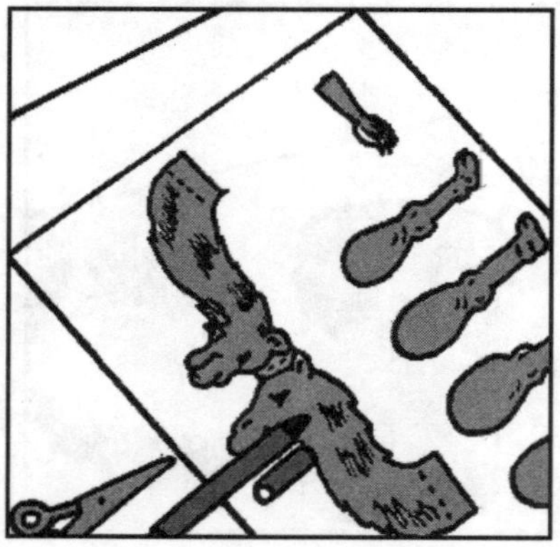

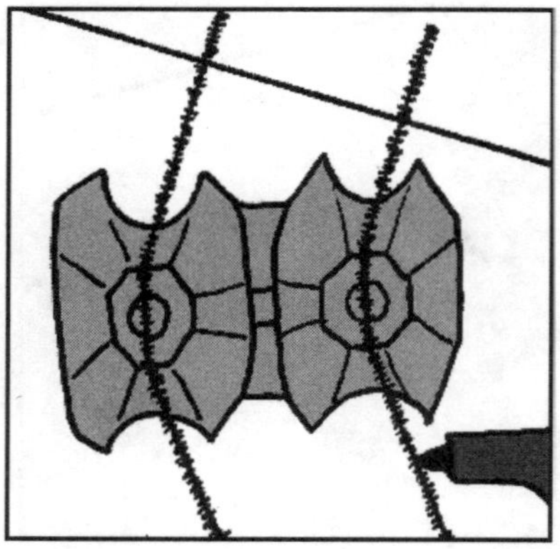

1 Cut out a two-cup secton from the egg carton. Spray paint two-cup egg section and let dry.

2 Color head, legs, and tail brown and cut out.

3 Cut two 10 ½" pipe cleaners and bend both in a **U** shape. Then glue the **U** shaped pipe cleaners inside the humps and let dry.

JANANNA TIPS	Egg cartons are great to hold scissors. Turn carton upside down and punch hole in bottom large enough for scissors to fit.

pipe cleaners

permanent markers or crayons

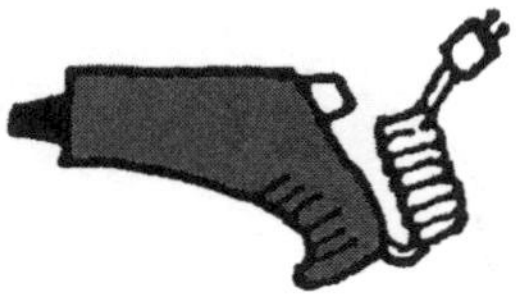

hot glue gun

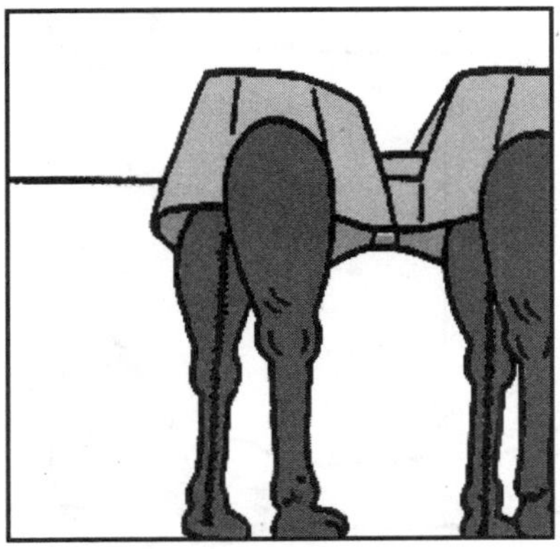

4 Attach leg pieces to pipe cleaners and humps and let dry.

5 Fold head and glue together to the fold line. Bend folds out. Then glue folds to one end of humps and let dry.

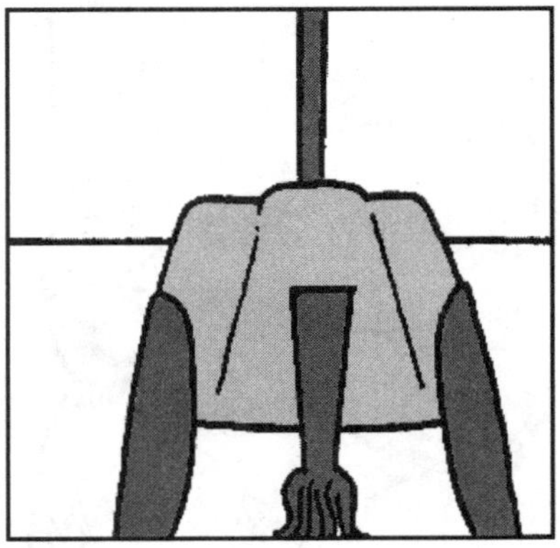

6 Glue tail piece to opposite end of the head and let dry.

CAMEL PATTERNS

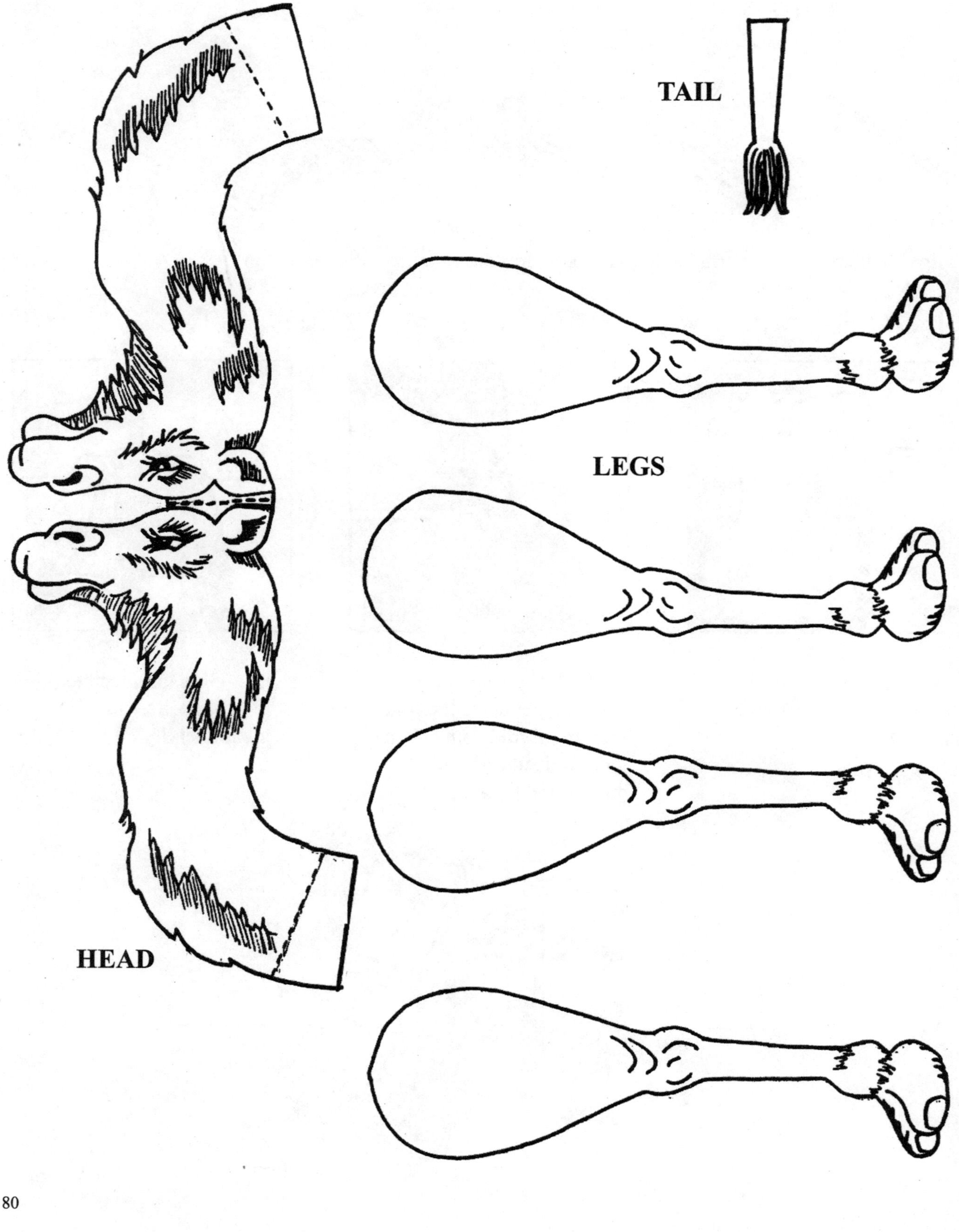